EUREKA!

EUREKA!

The Surprising Stories Behind
the Ideas That Shaped the World

MARLENE WAGMAN-GELLER

A PERIGEE BOOK

A PERIGEE BOOK
Published by the Penguin Group
Penguin Group (USA) Inc.
375 Hudson Street, New York, New York 10014, USA

Penguin Group (Canada), 90 Eglinton Avenue East, Suite 700, Toronto, Ontario M4P 2Y3,
Canada (a division of Pearson Penguin Canada Inc.) • Penguin Books Ltd., 80 Strand, London
WC2R 0RL, England • Penguin Group Ireland, 25 St. Stephen's Green, Dublin 2, Ireland (a
division of Penguin Books Ltd.) • Penguin Group (Australia), 250 Camberwell Road, Camber-
well, Victoria 3124, Australia (a division of Pearson Australia Group Pty. Ltd.) • Penguin Books
India Pvt. Ltd., 11 Community Centre, Panchsheel Park, New Delhi—110 017, India • Penguin
Group (NZ), 67 Apollo Drive, Rosedale, North Shore 0632, New Zealand (a division of Pearson
New Zealand Ltd.) • Penguin Books (South Africa) (Pty.) Ltd., 24 Sturdee Avenue, Rosebank,
Johannesburg 2196, South Africa

Penguin Books Ltd., Registered Offices: 80 Strand, London WC2R 0RL, England

While the author has made every effort to provide accurate telephone numbers and Internet
addresses at the time of publication, neither the publisher nor the author assumes any
responsibility for errors, or for changes that occur after publication. Further, the publisher does
not have any control over and does not assume any responsibility for author or third-party
websites or their content.

Copyright © 2010 by Marlene Wagman-Geller
Text design by Tiffany Estreicher

First edition: July 2010

Library of Congress Cataloging-in-Publication Data

Wagman-Geller, Marlene.
 Eureka! : the surprising stories behind the ideas that shaped the world / Marlene Wagman-
Geller.— 1st ed.
   p. cm.
 "A Perigee book."
 Includes bibliographical references.
 ISBN 978-0-399-53589-5
 1. Civilization, Modern—19th century—Anecdotes. 2. Civilization, Modern—20th century—
Anecdotes. 3. Intellectual life—History—19th century—Anecdotes. 4. Intellectual life—
History—20th century—Anecdotes. I. Title.
 CB417.W194 2010   909.08—dc22   2010002398

PRINTED IN THE UNITED STATES OF AMERICA
10 9 8 7 6 5 4 3 2 1

Once again to my J's . . . and to all eureka moments.

Introduction

Eureka! I found it!

—Archimedes of Syracuse, 287–212 BC

The field of etymology uncovers the genesis of words, and they often have colorful origins. One of our words came about when King Hiero II had concerns regarding his laurel leaf–shaped crown. He was worried about whether it was made of solid gold or whether the royal jewelers had added some base metal. The king turned the problem over to Archimedes, along with a caveat: The mathematician could not, as he conducted his investigation, damage the crown. After futilely pondering this conundrum, Archimedes stepped into his bathtub. When he did so, he noticed the water level rise. This led to his eureka moment: He could determine the density of the crown by noting how much water it displaced. He realized that if any other material had been added to the crown, it would be less dense than if it were made of solid gold. In his excitement, he ran naked through the streets of Syracuse shouting "Eureka!" which translates to "I have found it!" Since then, the expression has come to refer to aha moments, when one's intellectual lightbulb (oftentimes long elusive) miraculously flashes.

It would be ironic if in this volume on eurekas I did not include my own. After the completion of my first book, *Once Again to Zelda: The Stories Behind Literature's Most Intriguing Dedications*, I desperately desired to come up with an idea for a second book. However, as I deemed it a miracle I had thought of one publishable idea, I could not imagine ever coming up with another.

Yet one day, while driving to work, I had my own eureka. It was born from a frequent question I had received about *Zelda*: "How did you come up with the idea for your book?" This led to my realization: Everything originates with a creative spark; therefore, I could write a book exploring the stories behind the eureka moments that left an indelible mark on society. Just as I had been a dedication detective with *Zelda*, I now became a eureka detective.

Some of these catalysts I had already been familiar with, such as the stories behind two childhood classics: A. A. Milne was inspired by the stuffed animal of his son, Christopher Robin, and Winnie-the-Pooh was born; Ruth Handler was inspired by her daughter, Barbara, playing with paper-doll cutouts, and Barbie was created. As I started to do my research, I realized I was fascinated to unearth the histories behind the icons, and I hoped others would be as well.

I discovered that many eurekas were born when their creators were in foreign countries. This was the case when the French Madame Tussaud was in England, when the Bavarian Levi Strauss was in the United States, when the Belgian Gerard Blitz was in Corsica, and when the American Howard Schultz was in Italy.

However, eureka moments were not confined merely to foreign lands: *Jeopardy!* was born on an airplane, Penguin Books originated in a train station, Curious George was drawn as a result of a visit to a zoo, and the Seussian world was hatched aboard a ship.

Some of the eureka moments resulted in a heightened materialism: This was the case with one man who discovered an alternative nugget in the Gold Rush and another who turned a jumble of cheap items into a citadel of capitalism.

I discovered history's eureka moments from the Internet, books, and newspaper and magazine articles, and by just observing my everyday milieus. To be included in the book, the origin had to have been inspired by a eureka moment, famous enough to be considered part of contemporary cultural literacy, and with a backstory as intriguing (if not more) than the end result.

Sometimes I would track down a lead, only to discover that though the story behind it had a riveting origin, it did not owe its genesis to a lightbulb moment. This was the case with Whole Foods, which started from happenstance, not a hand-slap-to-the-forehead moment. Craigslist began in 1995 when Craig Newmark, a newcomer from New Jersey, started an email newsletter of local San Francisco events, in the hope of connecting with people. It mushroomed into an Internet giant; however, it could not be considered a eureka moment as it just naturally evolved and then escalated. Those stories, interesting as they may be, were not included, as they did not contain the requisite eureka moment.

Other stories had to be excluded because although they were born from eureka moments, not enough information was available about their creators. For instance, there is scant biographical information about Twitter creator Jack Dorsey (research only revealed a "tweet" amount of information), indicating either that his life story could be written on the head of a pin with room left over, or that he is extremely private.

On the Fields Medal for outstanding achievements in mathematics, there is a portrait of Archimedes. The inscription encircling the head of the mathematician is a quote attributed to him, in Latin: *Transire suum pectus mundoque potin* ("Rise above oneself and grasp the world"). Archimedes' quotation embodies the very essence of the eureka moment.

It is my heartfelt hope that reading about the famous eureka moments of history will result in your own.

Marlene Wagman-Geller
San Diego, California
2010

Postscript: Please email me at onceagaintozelda@hotmail.com to share any other famous eureka moments.

Eureka #1
(1772)

ronically, from one of the darkest chapters of history arose one of the greatest passages of light, thanks to a eureka moment that occurred off the coast of the appropriately named Newfoundland. The epiphany resulted in the salvation of a sinner and brought a state of grace to countless others.

John Newton's most devastating childhood trauma was when his beloved mother succumbed to tuberculosis. With her passing, he was bereft of the love and religious instruction she had lavished on him. He became bitter, rebellious, and angry, and on some level an orphan, as his father, John Newton Sr., was an unloving parent. Upon his father's remarriage, John was sent to a boarding school in Stratford, Essex. His education ended at age eleven, when his father, a commander of a merchant ship, arranged for him to exchange his studies for the sea. In order to secure a livelihood for his son, he arranged for John to become a slave master at a sugar plantation in Jamaica. When this fell through, John was forced into the royal naval service and became a midshipman aboard the HMS *Hardwich*.

Living conditions on the warship were deplorable; there was less room than in a prison, and the food was flavored with maggots. For diversion, there was always the imminent threat of death by enemy fire. Unable to tolerate the horror of his existence, John escaped. However, he was recaptured and court-martialed. To make an impression on his crew, the captain had the eighteen-year-old Newton stripped to the waist, where he received innumerable lashes until he fell into a coma. Further sadism involved pouring vinegar, salt water, and alcohol into his wounds. He was subsequently demoted from his position to that of a common seaman. The wretchedness of his life led Newton to contemplate suicide. After a while, he was traded to another captain, this one in charge of a slave ship bound for Sierra Leone. Wretched as life was for the common sailor, life for kidnapped slaves aboard passage to the Americas was even worse. Newton was to later recall of his days of trafficking humans, "I was sunk into complacency with the vilest of wretches."

As rebellious on the slave ship as he had been in the Royal Navy, Newton ironically ended up becoming the personal servant of a slave trader named Clow, whose African mistress had an intense dislike of John and encouraged the natives to jeer and throw rocks at her white slave. His clothes turned to rags, and he was forced to beg for survival. Eventually he was rescued from this nightmare by a sea captain who had ties with his father.

In time, Newton became the captain of his own Liverpool slave ship, the *Greyhound*, whereupon he took the first step on the road to his ultimate epiphany. In 1748, while sailing off the coast of Newfoundland, his vessel became tempest tossed, and each crew member felt that hour was to be his last. Mere moments after John left his position on the deck, the sailor who had taken his place was swept out to sea. As he frantically bailed out salt water, he realized his own human frailty and did something he had not done since the death of his mother: He prayed. He beseeched God to save him although he was a wretched blasphemer who had strayed far from a state of grace. When the storm abated, Newton took it as a sign of God's deliverance. For the rest of his life, he observed the date of his rescue as the day of his conversion, the time he began to subject his will to a higher power. He said of this, "The 10th of March is a day much to be remembered by me, and I have never suffered it to pass wholly unnoticed since the year 1748."

Another turn in his spiritual life was when, right after the storm, he chanced upon a book by Thomas à Kempis, *Imitation of Christ*, which further enmeshed him in evangelical Christianity. From this point on, he eschewed profanity, gambling, and drinking. In addition, he commanded his sailors to treat the bound captives with compassion.

On one of his stopovers in England, Newton married Mary Cartlett, with whom he had been in love since he was seventeen and she was fourteen. However, even the stability of a happy marriage was not enough for him to give up his position as a slave captain. As a trafficker of humans, he was not a poster boy of redemption.

Newton was on the coast of Guinea when he came down with a fever that almost claimed his life. After being saved from his second brush with death, John Newton had an epiphany; his task was to spend the remainder of his life in the abolition movement to end slavery. He felt that God had saved not only his life but also his soul, and claimed this experience was his true conversion and the turning point in his spiritual life.

John Newton returned to England a changed man, determined to spend the latter part of his life making amends for his prior wretchedness. He applied for a minister's position, and although not qualified, as he did not possess a university degree, the landlord of the parish of Olney, in Buckinghamshire, was so impressed with the letters that he penned about his spiritual conversion that he offered him a position at the Olney church, and John was ordained in 1764. He had traversed the road from sinner to a man of the cloth.

Newton spent the next sixteen years at his post, during which time his sermons were so mesmerizing his church erected a gallery to accommodate the throngs of people who flocked to hear him preach. He also worked with the abolitionist William Wilberforce and wrote a treatise, *Thoughts Upon the African Slave Trade*. In it, he called his old position "a business at which my heart now shudders."

It was also in Olney that the new curate met the poet William Cowper, also a newly born Christian. He helped Newton with his religious services; in addition, the two set up a series of Thursday evening prayer meetings, for which their goal was to write a new hymn each week. For one of these, written in Warwickshire for a Christmas service in 1772, John Newton had his eureka moment: He would compose a verse that would epitomize mankind's spiritual odyssey, one that would aid fellow pilgrims in pain. The result was one of the most beloved hymns in history, "Amazing Grace." The first verse encapsulated his freedom, metaphorically, from the shackles of evil:

> Amazing grace, how sweet the sound
> That sav'd a wretch like me!
> I once was lost, but now am found,
> Was blind, but now I see.

John Newton, in atonement for his forty years as a slave trader and self-proclaimed libertine, devoted himself to his pulpit and the emancipation of slaves. Even in the last year of his life, almost blind, he continued to preach, trying to save those who had yet to be found. When his friends suggested that the increasingly feeble minister retire, the specter of his past, like Marley's ghost, arose, and he replied in a ringing voice, perhaps to drown out the roar of the remembered sea, "I cannot stop. What? Shall the old African blasphemer stop while he can speak?" His last sermon, during which he had to be reminded of his subject, was for the widows and orphans of the Battle of Trafalgar of 1806. At age eighty-two, he said, "My memory is nearly gone, but I remember two things. That I am a great sinner, and that Christ is a great savior." He had at last achieved the title of his most memorable hymn.

Newton passed away in London the following year, where he was interred by the side of his wife, in St. Mary Woolmoth. Eventually, they were laid to rest in their old parish of Olney. He made his transition from this world to the next secure in his belief that his God would lead him home.

- "Amazing Grace" was popular on both sides in the American Civil War.
- Harriet Beecher Stowe, in *Uncle Tom's Cabin*, quoted three stanzas of the hymn.
- The hymn became a part of America's cultural literacy in large part because of the 1969 film *Alice's Restaurant*, in which Lee Hayes of the Weavers leads worshippers in singing "Amazing Grace."
- Newton was portrayed by the actor Albert Finney in the 2006 film *Amazing Grace*. The film portrayed Newton as a penitent who was haunted by the ghosts of 20,000 slaves.
- Newton was an extensive journalist and letter writer. Historians accredit his writings for much of what is known about the eighteenth-century British slave trade.

Eureka #2
(1836)

Because of a eureka moment, a housekeeper's daughter was to become the hostess of seven palatial establishments, each of which hosts visitors from the ranks of the famous and the infamous. Furthermore, this grande dame of the world's most remarkable salons had a life story that rivals even that of her world-renowned guests.

Anne Made Grosholz had to deal with being a new mother and widow when her soldier husband, Joseph, was killed in battle. Moreover, she had to do so with no income, as her spouse's salary had been the family's sole source of revenue. Fortunately, she was able to secure employment as a housekeeper for Dr. Philippe Curtius, who took the mother and her daughter, Marie, with him from France to Berne, Switzerland.

Dr. Curtius was interested in wax models, which he used to illustrate anatomy. The young Marie, who called her mother's employer "uncle," therefore grew up in a household where it was not unusual to see random body parts. When Dr. Curtius returned to Paris, he again took Anne and Marie with him.

Marie, after serving as an apprentice, soon showed such remarkable talent that he began to let her undertake sittings on her own. While other sixteen-year-old girls were courting handsome, eligible boys, Marie was busy immortalizing Jean-Jacques Rousseau, Voltaire, and Benjamin Franklin. After Marie and Dr. Curtius had created a number of figures, he made an exhibition of their craft at the Palais Royal in 1776. This was so successful that he staged another at the Boulevard du Temple, which he called the Caverne des Grands Voleurs. This one, perhaps in response to the growing violence in Paris, was more of a chamber of horrors than a portrait gallery.

Because Marie was so masterful in her art, she received a summons requesting her to move into the palace in order to tutor King Louis' sister, Madame Elizabeth. Consequently, Marie and her mother lived in one of the most magnificent estates of Europe. However, outside the rarified mirrored walls of the palace, a tidal wave of violence was fast approaching. On July 12, an infuriated mob marched on Versailles. At the front of the procession were the wax heads of Jacques Necker and the Duc d' Orleans, which had been raided from Dr. Curtius' exhibit. Two days later, the peasants stormed into the opulent residence and not only arrested King Louis, Marie Antoinette, and the rest of the royals but Marie and Anne Grosholz as well; the latter two were sent to La Force Prison.

Although they tried to reason with their captors that Marie was merely a royal employee who had been compelled to tutor the princess, and that Anne was a former housekeeper, their pleas fell on deaf ears. The architects of the

Reign of Terror were not known for their powers of reason. The women were thrown into a cell, one which they shared with Josephine de Beauharnais, who later became the love of Napoleon Bonaparte's life. Mother and daughter (along with the future empress) had their heads shaven for their appointment with Madame Guillotine. Frantically, Marie tried to contact Philippe Curtius, but he had left the country. However, he did in the end prove to be her savior, just not in the way she had envisioned.

Realizing their prisoner was the famous wax maker, the Revolutionaries made her a Faustian bargain: If she made death masks of the beheaded, they would spare her life and her mother's. Marie agreed, though some of the victims were those with whom she had lived for nine years.

When the Reign of Terror ended, Marie married a younger man, François Tussaud, with whom she had two sons, Joseph and François. Her husband squandered her inheritance from Philippe Curtius, leaving her destitute. At a time when the only independent businesswomen were those who sold their flesh, she decided to peddle another form of flesh, one made of wax. She took her uncle's figures on tour; she was never to see her homeland or husband again.

She and her sons and their wax heads toured Britain and Ireland for the next thirty-three years. On one tour en route to Ireland, the ship carrying much of her collection capsized in a storm. Perhaps seeing the disembodied faces of people she had sculpted bobbing on the surface of their watery graves brought back a gory reminder of when she had been forced to sit at the base of the guillotine, searching through a basket of freshly severed heads.

At age seventy-four, Marie found the task of endlessly packing and repacking her wax models increasingly exhausting. Moreover, the sea voyages brought to mind her earlier capsizing trauma, and her figures were always in danger of destruction on the bumpy Georgian roads. However, she was not willing to forgo her career, as it was her life's grand passion. It was at this juncture that Marie had her eureka moment: She decided that she would establish a new kind of museum—one that would permanently display her waxworks. In this way, she would also be able to create elaborate backdrops. She found a location for her display on Baker Street in London. Her one-of-a-kind exhibit met with great success, one that eighteenth-century women rarely achieved in the business world. For the first time people could see, other than in print, the newsmakers of their era. Along with displaying the prominent figures of her time, she also included the death's heads from the Revolution, replete with an authentic blade from the guillotine. Remembering the great success of her uncle Philippe's Caverne des Grands Voleurs, she re-created the chamber of horrors.

At age seventy-seven, Marie wrote her memoirs. Most of the autobiography, however, deals with the well-known people and famous events that had so impacted her life. When it came to her own story, Ms. Tussaud was more reticent. Except for her two sons, mother, and adopted uncle, she had rarely formed any other important attachments. Perhaps she felt more at ease with those of wax than with those of flesh.

In the front entrance of her museum in London, she created a self-portrait of herself in her eighties, in the act of taking money from customers. This exhibit is still on display, so real that one is tempted to ask her the price of admission. It depicts a black-clad, unsmiling woman: She had seen too much horror to have any other expression on her waxen face. On vigil at her deathbed were her two sons. Her last words to them proved that her wisdom was not merely confined to wax: "I divide my property equally between you, and implore you, above all things, never to quarrel." Because of a French-woman's eureka moment in Britain, the world began its cult of celebrity. It also served to make Madame Tussaud's hundred-year-old establishment one of London's crown jewels, and her name forever associated with the medium in which she was the undisputed queen.

- The Las Vegas museum has interactive figures. Whisper into Jennifer Lopez's ear and she will blush; hold Elvis' hand and he will speak in his famous Southern drawl.
- The London branch of Madame Tussauds is the city's chief tourist attraction, drawing 2.8 million visitors a year.
- The museum's most photographed exhibit is Arnold Schwarzenegger.
- The only person who has refused a wax likeness is Mother Teresa.
- A curator at the London Madame Tussauds explained that they had to use glue to fix one of its exhibits. The spokesperson explained, "Every time we passed by Bill Clinton's wax figure, the zipper was undone."

Eureka #3
(1871)

I t is embraced by people from every social stratum and has been partnered with a great many names and symbols. Although typically American, it was originally associated with two Europeans, men whose creation became the origin of the popular trend.

Jacob Youphes left Latvia for America in 1831. Although never able to change his thick accent, he was able to change his name, which became Jacob Davis. He eventually settled in Nevada, where he opened up a tailor shop to support his wife and six children. His chief business was in making wagon covers and tents from an off-white cotton called duck cloth, which he purchased from the wholesale house of another immigrant who hailed from Bavaria.

Loeb Strauss immigrated on steerage to New York, where he joined his two older siblings in their dry-goods business, J. Strauss Brother & Co. The young Loeb learned the trade and often walked the streets as an itinerant peddler. However, as an observant Jew, he always returned to Manhattan in time for the

Friday Sabbath. When the cry came out, "There's gold in them thar hills!" he decided to become part of the exodus streaming west. Although he did not know it at the time, he was going to discover gold, just not in a way he ever envisioned. He opened up his own business under his nickname, Levi (which he often went by), and it grew so prosperous that he became one of the burgeoning city's chief philanthropists and founded Temple Emanu-El, San Francisco's first synagogue.

Strauss and Davis would have been swallowed in the annals of Ellis Island history except for an ordinary event, one that was to forever change their lives and, in a fashion, that of America. In 1870, a customer came to Jacob, asking for a "cheap" pair of pants for her "large" husband, Alkali Ike. She had a complaint common to many of the miners and their spouses: When they found their gold nuggets, they placed them in their pockets for safekeeping, which quickly tore under the strain. She paid him $3 for the pair in advance and begged him to make them as strong as possible. Her comment triggered Jacob's eureka moment: He decided to reinforce his pants' pockets and button fly with the copper rivets he used to attach straps to horse blankets. They were a success, so much so that within a year and a half he had sold two hundred pairs. However, he became alarmed when other tailors began to pirate his brainchild. He was desperate to apply for a patent but did not have the requisite $68. He needed a partner and immediately thought of his fabric supplier in San Francisco, Levi Strauss. Jacob wrote a letter outlining his invention and suggesting that the two men take out a patent together. Strauss, an astute businessman, immediately grasped the potential.

On May 20, 1873, they received a patent for "Improvement in Fastening Pocket Openings" (#139,121). It was to become the official birthday of what would later be termed "blue jeans." In the same year, Davis pasted on the rear pocket an orange-threaded double arc design (the color was chosen to match the color of the rivets) to distinguish them from their competitors; it is the oldest apparel trademark still in use today. Another innovation was that the white duck cloth was replaced with denim dyed with indigo, so that the miner's dirt could better be camouflaged. In 1886, Levi sewed a leather label on the back of the pants, with a picture of a pair of jeans pulled by two horses, a visual symbol of the strength of the new riveted pants. An American icon had been launched. Levis became the jeans that won the West.

The partnership between the two men proved to be the start of a beautiful friendship. Strauss invited Davis to move to San Francisco to oversee the manufacturing of the riveted pants that would soon become the main focus of Levi Strauss & Co. One style, known then as XX, now known as 501, became a bestseller. At the onset, the pants were sewn by women in their homes, but the demand was such that the men opened up a factory, with Davis acting as foreman. Long after the gold dried up, the pants still flourished, becoming an American clothing staple and making the House of Levi a fashion icon. The two immigrants turned denim, thread, and metal into the most popular item of clothing in the world.

Levi Strauss passed away in 1902, and his death was headline news in the *San Francisco Call*. On the day of his funeral, local businesses closed so that the owners could attend his funeral. The eulogy was read at Strauss' home by Rabbi Jacob

Voorsanger of the temple that Strauss had founded. Levi Strauss, who had never married or had children, left the bulk of his $6 million to his four nephews, as well as various charitable organizations. Although the Levi Strauss factory was destroyed by the fire that raged in the aftermath of the 1906 earthquake, it was rebuilt by Levi's nephews. Similarly, the four boys proved that they were their uncle's spiritual heirs; they continued to pay their employees' salaries until the plant was rebuilt.

The pants initiated by Jacob and Levi traveled from the 49ers panning for gold to the cowboys riding to their home on the range to Rosie the Riveter shouting, "We can do it!" to Marlon Brando calling "Stella!" to Brooke Shields' seductive "Nothing gets between me and my Calvins" to Neil Diamond's love song "Forever in Blue Jeans." What would the two Jewish Old World merchants have thought if they could have foreseen that their waist overalls would one day be intricately enmeshed in the chronicles of America?

- In 1964, a pair of Levis jeans entered the permanent collection of the Smithsonian Institution in Washington, DC.
- Genovese sailors made the first pants from the material and so the pants were named "genes," which was Americanized to "jeans."
- In 1920, the button-up front was replaced with a zipper. In 1936, the red tab was created to identify the brand from a distance.
- In 1997, Levi Strauss & Co. paid $25,000 for a pair of hundred-year-old jeans (for their museum) that had been discovered in a Colorado mine. It is the oldest known pair of Levis.

Eureka #4
(1872)

When a blue blood journeyed from his bluegrass state to England, a eureka moment resulted that imbued his journey with far greater implications than the customary jaunt abroad.

The Lewis and Clark expedition connotes the era when Thomas Jefferson transacted the Louisiana Purchase from Napoleon Bonaparte as part of America's Manifest Destiny. The intrepid adventurers Meriwether Lewis and William Clark, along with their female Native American guide, Sacagawea, explored the unchartered territory, and their historic journey became part of Old West lore. Seventy-one years later, Clark's grandson, named after Clark's fellow adventurer, would also bequeath his country a legend.

When Meriwether Lewis Clark Jr. was six years old, his mother, Abigail Prather Churchill, passed away, and Lutie, as he was nicknamed, went to live with his maternal uncles, John and Henry, whose wealth and prestige made them one of the First Families of Kentucky. Living with his affluent relatives, the young man acquired a taste for expensive things, such as custom-made suits, good food, champagne, and horse racing.

In 1872, Lutie went on a trip to England, where he visited the country's famous Epsom Derby. While attending one of its races, Clark had his eureka moment: He would re-create in Kentucky the race he had witnessed in Europe. His homeland had superior horses, a result of their feeding on the indigenous bluegrass, and his relatives could provide the requisite money and connections to turn his brainchild into a reality. Fired with enthusiasm, he visited the French Jockey Club, which had organized the prestigious Grand Prix de Paris. Now all he had to do was convince his city's gentry that if they built a prestigious track, the world would beat a path to Kentucky's door.

Lutie's passion was met with a lukewarm reception. The people of Louisville, a city of 100,000 people, pointed out that it did not have a thriving economy and therefore could not support a superfluous hobby. Others stated that their southern town could not compete with New York, with its famous Saratoga track. Clark's massive frame matched his massive resolve, one that would not allow a door to be slammed in the face of his vision. One of the tactics he used was to appeal to Kentucky pride. He pointed out that New Orleans had Mardi Gras and Cincinnati (which Louisvillians loathed) had its music festival. Louisville's native horses could give their city a plane on which to compete. Grudgingly, some began to agree.

Two years later, Louisville's moneyed elite, composed of local bankers, hotel men, and streetcar-company owners, as well as local politicians, met with Meriwether Lewis Clark Jr. at Galt House, a luxurious hotel, with the end result being that the Louisville Jockey Club came into existence. Its primary function would be building the track and overseeing the operation of the ensuing races. At the close of the gathering, 320 people became charter members, each contributing a sum of $100. For his part, after securing the capital, Clark went on an extensive personal tour around his state to cajole citizens to patronize his derby. With the $32,000, Clark leased eighty acres from his uncles; the club would eventually be christened Churchill Downs in their honor.

In May 1875, the Colonel, as he was called, organized the initial race, drawing heavily on what he had learned in England. In tribute, he named his race the Kentucky Derby after the Epsom Derby. Its debut fell on a Monday; most stores had locked their doors, as astute businesses knew the only money that was going to change hands on that day was at the new track. Horse-drawn buggies and mule-drawn trolley cars caused congestion on the streets. The grandstands, which had been constructed to hold two thousand people, could not accommodate the crowd of ten thousand.

In Clark's clubhouse, the wealthy patrons sipped mint juleps, a classic Southern beverage imbibed from sterling silver cups, which were to evolve into a derby tradition. They enjoyed the spectacle from rockers on a veranda while Strauss waltzes played. Later the veranda would be transformed into Millionaire's Row, where the women would sport the most flamboyant and elegant of hats. A later ritual would come at the start of each race, when Stephen Foster's "My Old Kentucky Home" would be played.

The horses were started from a line drawn in the dirt across the track, and a drummer was used to alert the jockeys (all of whom, except one, were African American) that the race was about to begin. The winning horse, who rode into legend, was the three-year-old Aristides, whose owner received $2,900 for the victory.

The event later became referred to as the Run for the Roses. This tradition was initiated when New York socialite E. Berry Wall presented roses to ladies at a post-derby party in 1883. His actions led to Clark's idea of making roses the race's official flower. Later winners would be presented with a garland made of 564 red roses, which weighs thirty-five pounds. Now, 2,100 roses decorate the winner's circle.

Unfortunately, what harmed Clark the most was his own personality, which always ran neck and neck with his intelligence. His mercurial temper was perpetually ready to explode, a fact that contributed to the demise of his marriage. On one occasion, Lutie threatened the prominent breeder T. G. Moore with a gun and ordered him out of his Galt House office after having knocked him down in a dispute over fees. In retaliation, Moore got his own gun, which he fired at Clark through a door. The bullet landed in Clark's chest, lodging under his arm. His assailant subsequently turned himself in to the police, although no charges were brought.

For the next few years the Kentucky Derby was the success its founder had envisioned it to be. Clark busied himself with designing elaborate fanfares for his wealthy patrons, and his place became the watering hole for high society. Unfortunately, Lutie's focus on the upper crust came with a cost; track operations were left to incompetent subordinates, and Churchill Downs never showed a profit. Further trouble arose when James Ben Ali Haggin, a high-rolling New York patron, boycotted the derby over a slight from Clark; moreover, he convinced his fellow eastern horsemen to do likewise. Consequently, interest in the track plummeted, and it fell further into debt. Clark struggled on without pay, covering costs out of pocket. By 1894, the *Louisville Commercial* was referring to the derby as "a contest of dogs." The Colonel suffered further financial loss in the stock market crash of 1893.

Clark began traveling from city to city, working at various regional tracks. While in Chicago, a bartender at Clark's hotel took offense when Clark called Chicagoans "thieves and liars" and had words with him. Clark took off and returned with a gun, which he rested on the man's chest until he apologized. As there were a number of witnesses, the story was reported in both Chicago and Louisville newspapers. The Churchill brothers were not at all pleased with the resultant publicity. In their wills, they disinherited their nephew, leaving him no part of the track that he had dreamed into existence. Lutie committed suicide with a pistol on April 22, 1899. He was buried in Cave Hill Cemetery next to his uncle John Churchill, under a blanket of bluegrass.

Although the visionary died in ignominy, his vision was destined to become the crown jewel of horse races, and not just in the bluegrass state. The Kentucky Derby has been aptly named the Most Exciting Two Minutes in Sports. A century after Lutie's passing, 140,000 people flock to his old Kentucky home on the first Saturday of May, to pay homage to his eureka moment. To Lutie, they should tip their whimsical derbies and raise their silver mint julep glasses.

- The Kentucky Derby trophy is the only solid 14-karat gold one in American sports. It is topped with an 18-karat gold horse. It becomes the property of the winning owner.
- About 120,000 mint juleps, the derby's official drink, are served annually.
- The fastest time ever reached in the Kentucky Derby was set in 1973, when Secretariat clocked in at 1:59:40.
- A Thoroughbred horse is depicted on the back side of the Kentucky state quarter.
- The Kentucky Derby is the longest running sporting event in the United States. The horses have run without interruption since 1875, even during both world wars.

Eureka #5
(1879)

A proverb states, "Mighty oaks from little acorns grow." This was the case with a eureka moment that began with a table covered with a red cloth and resulted in a citadel to capitalism.

Franklin Winfield Woolworth, nicknamed Wooley, grew up on a potato farm in Rodham, New York. In the evenings, the family gathered, and his mother, Fanny, would give Wooley and his younger brother, Charles Sumner, lessons on the family's upright piano, its keys yellow with age.

The days, however, consisted of endless chores, all hateful to Wooley. From sunrise to sundown, he pitched hay, coaxed potatoes from the frozen ground, and shoveled endless piles of manure. As much as Wooley hated farming tools, he was fascinated by the trinkets of local peddlers, from whose packs appeared shiny pots, pans, and perfumed soaps. However, Fanny, a no-frills Methodist, was not likewise enticed.

Occasionally Wooley and Charles, along with their parents, would visit local stores. These outings proved a bittersweet experience: sweet because Wooley loved the milieu; bitter because he and Charles had only a few pennies to spend, and the salespeople looked with disdain at the family with threadbare clothing.

On rare days free from farm chores, Wooley and Charles' favorite pastime was visiting Old Nap's Place, as Wooley called the nearby abandoned estate that had once been owned by Joseph Bonaparte, the oldest brother of Napoleon, compliments of his megalomaniacal sibling.

At age twenty, Wooley applied for a job at a dry-goods store, determined to escape the poverty of his potato farm; he'd had his fill of calluses and blisters. He worked free for the first three months because as owner William Moore said, "Why should I pay you for teaching you the business?" A deal was made and so was history.

To be a salesman, Wooley had a lot to learn: In the mid-1870s, all items were locked up, and complicated price codes had to be retrieved or memorized. Moreover, there often was not even a set price; the salesperson and customer had to bargain. At this time, Wooley fell in love with Jennie Creighton, who had come to New York from Canada to search for employment as a seamstress. They met when she came into Wooley's store to buy sewing supplies. The couple married and had three daughters: Helena Maud, Edna, and Jessie May.

One auspicious morning, Wooley's boss told him to place a variety of items on an old sewing table, all of which would be sold for five cents. Wooley covered the table with red cloth (his favorite color) and arranged the cheap items as attractively as he could. The five-cent table caused a sensation, as crowds bought up the low-priced goods until they were all sold. The experience led to Wooley's eureka moment: a vision of a new kind of store where everything could be sold for five cents.

Enthusiastic over his epiphany, he convinced Moore to loan him $300 to open a store on a back street in Utica, New York. Within a few weeks, the business died, but his dream did not. He was not willing to go back to hoeing potatoes. And he had learned from the experience—location was essential—and so his next venture would be in the heart of a town, on its main street. He left Utica with $30 in his pocket and boundless ambition.

His next store was in Lancaster, Pennsylvania, which also carried merchandise for ten cents; with this business, the first successful five-and-dime store was born. Wooley proudly emblazoned his legal name on its entrance against a background of red: F. W. Woolworth. When his father viewed the store, he gave his oft-repeated comment to his son, "It's nice, Frank. You always did like to lay it on thick." And just as Napoleon had shared his spoils of empire with his brother Joseph, so Wooley did with his brother, Charles. Together they became partners, and by 1911, their company included 586 stores.

One ingenious idea of the merchant prince was to put a lunch counter in his stores, so that shopping would be a multifaceted experience. Each location had a gray Formica counter and spinning, red vinyl stools. They became the great gathering place on main streets throughout the country.

Franklin Woolworth decided to use his nickel-and-dime fortune as an alchemist's stone, one that would turn his red blood blue: His clothes were sewn by a European tailor, his vacations were in Europe, his chauffeur was a Grand Prix winner. His mansion, Winfield House in Long Island, had grounds that required seventy full-time gardeners, and the fifty-six-room mansion had dozens of servants. Its décor was heavily influenced by French architecture, in keeping with his fascination with the house of Napoleon. A huge pipe organ was also installed, a tribute to his mother's lessons at the potato farm. Woolworth, notoriously careful with his employees' salaries, spared no expense on his mansion: Its pink marble staircase cost $2 million.

However, the edifice for which he is best remembered is one of the first skyscrapers—the Woolworth Building in New York City, which became the crown jewel of capitalism. It was erected at a cost of $13.5 million, paid for in cash, and for many years was the tallest structure in the world. During its opening extravaganza, a reporter overheard the following exchange: "How did he do it?" one charwoman asked. "'Twas easy," replied the second, "with your dime and mine." Franklin's private office was patterned after Napoleon's Empire Room at Compiègne. The pièce de résistance was a life-size bust of Napoleon, which had once been owned by the emperor himself. A huge portrait of Bonaparte in his coronation robes hung opposite the mahogany and gilt desk. One can imagine Franklin's father's apparition saying, "It's nice, Frank. You always did like to lay it on thick."

However, even all of Woolworth's power, prestige, and privilege could not shield against disaster. Jennie was slowly slipping into senility, and his middle daughter, distraught over her philandering husband, committed suicide in the Plaza Hotel. Her body was discovered by her five-year-old daughter, Barbara Hutton. To compensate, Franklin lavished on her all that a fortune of nickels and dimes could buy. When she was eighteen, he threw her a multimillion-dollar ball in New York City. Outside the glittering soiree, endless lines of Depression-era homeless eyed the festivities; it was the Woolworth version of "Let them eat cake." Partly because of Barbara's debutante ball, the Woolworth lunch counter girls went on strike. To help alleviate the situation, the heiress was shipped off to one of the family's European mansions until an agreement between management and workers could be reached. When she turned twenty-one, she received $50 million (the equivalent of $1 billion today). After her seven divorces and several suicide attempts, the press dubbed her "poor little rich girl."

Ironically, the undoing of the man who had created the largest sweet shops in the world was his teeth. Because of a phobia of dentists, developed after his old employer, Moore, passed away from complications from oral surgery, Woolworth succumbed to an infection in his mouth. As he lay dying in Winfield House, Jennie, who had over the years retreated into a private world of dementia, sat endlessly rocking.

With the demise of the merchant prince, the giant chain began to close down. When it was time to shut the Greensboro outlet, the counter and its stools were given to the Smithsonian Institution. The Woolworth five-and-dime empire morphed into the Foot Locker, but the memory of the store had become an integral part of American nostalgia. Perhaps the most extraordinary aspect of the Woolworth story is that its eureka began with the most ordinary of things, an old sewing table filled with cheap items in a small-town dry-goods store.

- In the Grand Arcade of the Woolworth Building, a fresco was set into the second-floor balcony. It is believed that the face on the fresco was modeled after Franklin's beloved mother, Fanny.
- In 1918 alone, a billion people entered Woolworth's stores, and more than 820,000,000 bought goods.
- In 1938, a wallet was sold with a plastic cover to illustrate how well a Social Security card would fit in it. The store used a card with the actual number of one of its secretaries. Several thousand of them were sold, and as it turned out, thousands of people ended up using the secretary's number as their own. For tax reasons, it appeared that the secretary had millions of dollars. Ultimately, the number had to be voided, and the secretary was issued a new one.
- Until the 1970s, all Woolworth's store managers were male.

Eureka #6
(1883)

Once ideas are born, they develop a will of their own and oftentimes travel far from what their originators had initially conceived. Such is the case with a nineteenth-century eureka, in which an aristocrat decided to reform his country's educational system and ended up resurrecting a giant that had slumbered for 1,500 years.

Pierre de Coubertin was raised in Paris in a wealthy and cultured family. When he was eight years old, he lived through the defeat of his homeland in the Franco-Prussian War, which planted in him the idea that his nation's lack of physical education in its schools contributed to the defeat of France by Otto von Bismark. At that juncture, Pierre was a fan of a British novel for boys, *Tom Brown's School Days*, which stressed the importance of physical strength. He believed that if France had followed the British example of training its youth through exercise and sport, there would have been a different victor.

As a member of the aristocracy, Pierre indulged in a playboy lifestyle in Parisian society. However, despite his easy life (or because of it), he decided to be more than a member of the idle rich. Recalling his childhood conviction of French society's Achilles' heel during the war, he became determined to reform its educational system. Accordingly, he traveled to England to observe their physical education programs, feeling it was the reason the sun never set on the British Empire.

In 1890, after seven years of research, the baron visited Much Wenlock in Shropshire, where Dr. William Penny Brooks had put together a local revival of the Olympic Games. It proved a revelation to the twenty-seven-year-old, who saw it as the embodiment of the ideals of which he had dreamed. This led to his eureka moment: Olympics could serve as a rallying point not just for French schools but for the world. He determined to embark on a quest to bring about a revival of the Greek games.

In 1892, at a gathering of sports officials, de Coubertin enthusiastically outlined his brainchild, founded on the premise that it would foster a sense of universal brotherhood. The officials looked at him as if to say he should stick to the life of leisure. To them it was ludicrous to resume a pagan ritual, one in which athletes participated naked and women spectators were thrown from the cliffs of Mount Typaion to their deaths. The baron was only temporarily derailed.

In 1894, de Coubertin organized an international meeting of sportsmen, where seventy-nine delegates from nine countries attended. He argued that the games would provide a venue to ease world tensions; by the end of the Paris Congress, de Coubertin had formed the International Olympic Committee (IOC) in a ceremony held at the University of Sorbonne.

The founder's philosophy was embodied in what became the Olympic creed: "The most important thing in the Olympic Games is not to win but to take part, just as the most important thing in life is not the triumph but the struggle. The essential thing is not to have conquered but to have fought well." The members determined the first games should be symbolically held in Athens, on the foundation of the long-vanished Panathenan Stadium.

In 1896, the Olympic Games were reborn, 1,500 years after being panned by the Roman Emperor Theodosius I as a heathen rite. In attendance were King Georgios I and a crowd of 60,000 spectators. The king handed each victor a wreath of wild olive plucked from the trees of Olympia.

As the president of the Olympic Committee, the baron dedicated his life to refining his dream. He kept some traditions of the ancient games: They would be held every four years, and women would be excluded as participants, as he felt they were the delicate sex. Another revival was the Olympic flame. The Greeks considered fire a gift of Prometheus from the Gods and therefore sacred. A long relay of runners would carry the torch to the site of the host country. There it would light a cauldron that would remain lit until the closing ceremony.

Some innovations to the ancient model included holding the games in different countries and changing the underlying motif from the glory of Zeus to the glory of man: Its Latin motto was *Citius–Altius–Fortius*, or "Faster–Higher–Stronger." In addition, his fervent hope was that it would instill not merely national pride but also international brotherhood. This is why doves, a universal symbol of peace, are released after the cauldron is lit. To design the Olympic flag, de Coubertin turned to Greece, a country that had intrigued him ever since a German archaeologist had unearthed the ruins at Olympia. On a visit to Delphi, the baron had discovered an emblem of five linked rings on an ancient altar. He thought this symbolized the concept of the five continents, separate and yet connected by the games. From this was born the Olympic emblem, its colors containing all of the hues of the flags of the participating nations.

If Baron Pierre de Coubertin were still alive, he would be amazed at the road on which his idea has traveled. The pageantry of the 2008 Beijing Olympics became a $100 million extravaganza. Women proved not to be the delicate sex when, at the 1976 Montreal games, Romanian Nadia Comaneci became the first gymnast to be awarded a perfect mark of 10.00. (Unequipped for this contingency, the scoreboards registered 1.00.)

However, in other ways, the founding father would have been devastated at some of the negative paths his brainchild trod. In 1916, the Olympic headquarters moved from France to the neutral Switzerland because of World War I, and two games had to be canceled in the 1940s because of World War II. In 1936, Hitler turned the Munich games into a venue for Nazi propaganda, and swastikas outnumbered the interlocking rings. Tragically, during the 1972 games in Munich, Palestinian terrorists murdered eleven members of the Israeli wrestling team.

Personal misfortune also dogged de Coubertin's final days. As an infant, his son suffered severe sunstroke, which left him in a catatonic state, and his daughter was plagued with mental disorders that required lifelong care. A further heartache was the death of his sister-in-law and two nephews, who perished in the war.

Baron Pierre de Coubertin died of a sudden heart attack in Geneva while he was strolling in a park. After his passing, one final Olympic ritual was carried out. In accordance with his will, his body was interned in Lausanne, as it was the seat of the International Olympic Committee, but his heart was removed and buried near the ruins of ancient Olympia, under a marble monument the Greeks had erected in his honor. Each year, when the torch is lit, the first runner en route to the host city stops in Coubertin Grove in homage.

De Coubertin never reformed the French educational system; however, he ignited a torch that still enlightens, and his interlocking rings still hold the promise to unite a fractured world.

- Statues of de Coubertin were erected in Atlanta and in Lausanne, France.
- Until 1908, the marathon standard had been set at exactly twenty-six miles. However, at the Olympic marathon in London, the royal family wanted a better view of the finish line, so organizers added an extra 385 yards to the race so that the finish line would be in front of the royal box.
- The Olympic flame in Olympia is rekindled every two years using the sun's rays and a concave reflective mirror.
- An iconic image of the games is Jesse Owens saluting the American flag while Hitler's Aryan athletes are giving the Nazi salute.

Eureka #7
(1888)

Marc Antony, when he delivered Caesar's funeral oration, stated, "The evil that men do lives after them; the good is oft interred with their bones." One man, because of his errant brainchild, knew his unwitting legacy would be evil; however, because of his eureka moment, he was able to ensure that his goodness did not perish when he died.

Alfred Bernhard Nobel was born in Sweden in 1833. Although he was interested in pursuing a career in the arts, he was dissuaded by his father, Immanuel, who was determined that his offspring become engineers in the family business. Their focus was to work with nitroglycerine in order to make the deadly substance more controlled.

There was a humanitarian reason behind their efforts. The highly volatile liquid was resulting in a vast number of workmen's deaths. Tragically, during experimentation, an explosion claimed four workers' lives as well as the youngest Nobel son, Emil. The shock caused Immanuel to have a stroke.

At age thirty-one, as Alfred was lifting a bottle of nitroglycerine, he accidentally spilled some on packing material,
which consisted of a fine powder. However, instead of explod-
ing, the two coalesced and created a paste. He realized he had
stumbled on an important discovery: The mixture was still
explosive but much safer to handle. He christened his discovery "dynamite." As companies blasted out rocks for railroads,
tunnels, and canals across America, India, and Panama, the
shy scientist, also an astute businessman, opened factories in
ninety locations in more than twenty countries.

Alfred moved his base to his favorite city, Paris. However,
the restless man was seldom at rest, and he constantly traveled from one of his six homes, which were in six countries, to
another. Victor Hugo described him as "Europe's richest
vagabond." In each of his residences he built a factory, as he
was a lifelong workaholic. He said, "My home is where I work
and I work everywhere."

Unfortunately, the successful businessman was not successful in his personal life. Intense work and travel, coupled
with his extremely introverted nature, had not been conducive to romance. His personality, always melancholic, further
exacerbated his single status. For example, when a relative
asked for a contribution toward their family history, he replied, "Greatest sin: does not worship Mammon. Important
events in his life: none." Then, as an even more acerbic after-
thought, he added that he "should have been strangled by a
humanitarian doctor when he made his screeching entrance
into the world."

One of the only areas that brought Alfred pleasure was literature and creative writing, a career that his father had de-

railed. His library consisted of 1,500 volumes, which ranged from fiction to philosophy. In his unfinished novel, *Brothers and Sisters*, he wrote, "You say I am a riddle—it may be, for all of us are riddles unexplained."

At age forty-three, he placed an advertisement (perhaps one of the first personal columns) in a Vienna newspaper, ostensibly looking for someone to help him in his French palatial mansion. "Wealthy, highly educated elderly gentleman seeks lady of mature age, versed in languages, as secretary and supervisor of household." The woman who ended up in the position was thirty-three-year-old Austrian Bertha Kinsky. She immediately awakened in him feelings of affection, ones that he had formerly only felt toward his beloved mother. On her second day, he handed her a poem that he had written in his youth and later shyly asked her "if her heart was free." Tactfully she answered that she was already engaged and had taken the job to ensure a measure of economic independence.

During the time Bertha lived with Alfred, more in the capacity as a companion than a housekeeper, she interested him in the causes that were near and dear to her heart. One was her opposition to countries stockpiling munitions, a subject she attacked in her book *Lay Down Your Arms*. However, when she asked him to join her at an international peace conference, he refused. He insisted his explosives advanced the cause of peace faster than her congresses: "The day when two armies can annihilate each other in one second, all civilized nations will recoil from war in horror and disband their armies."

After a year she returned to Austria to marry Count Arthur von Suttner, but she remained one of Nobel's only friends. Bertha, who became Baroness von Suttner, was to become a prominent pioneer in the international organization for peace.

The event that altered Alfred's—and, to an extent, the world's—destiny was a premature obituary in an 1888 French newspaper. He was aghast when he read about his own demise. It stated, *Le marchand de la mort est mort* ("The Merchant of Death Is Dead"). It continued, saying the dynamite king, who had "become rich by finding ways to kill more people faster than ever before, died yesterday." In actuality, it had been Alfred's brother Ludwig who had passed away.

Alfred's first reaction was to counter the article by saying that his invention had made possible the Panama Canal and had saved countless workers' lives. However, he also realized that his brainchild had not been the weapon to end all wars, as he had told Bertha. He sadly acknowledged that dynamite had become one of the most deadly tools in the arsenal of destruction. Depressed that what he had devised to better humanity was contributing to its demise, and not desiring his legacy to be the "Merchant of Death," Alfred determined to find a way to make amends for the destruction his invention had wrought and to alter the way future generations would remember his name. However, how to do so proved the rub. Shortly thereafter, Alfred Nobel had his eureka moment: He would use the fruits of his dynamite-generated fortune to create an annual prize, one that would bear his name and reward those who made the greatest contributions to the betterment of the world.

His inspiration had come from Bertha, the only woman who had ever touched his isolated heart. In 1895, one of the world's richest men called a meeting with four witnesses in the Swedish Club of Paris, with the purpose of drawing up what was going to become the most famous last will and testament in history. He purposely did not have a lawyer present, as his opinion of them was low: "Lawyers have to make a living and can only do so by inducing people to believe that a straight line is crooked."

Nobel wrote his three-hundred-word document on a torn half sheet of paper and declared it his final will. In it he changed his former one, wherein he had left his fortune to his nieces and nephews. He explained his change of heart: "Inherited wealth is a misfortune which merely serves to dull man's faculties."

Instead, he bequeathed his 31 million kroner ($186 million today) to reward "those persons who shall have contributed most materially to the benefit of mankind during the year immediately preceding." In this way he felt that he would rewrite his epitaph to humanity. His final behest was a radical one, as up till that time all inheritances had gone to family, the church, or the poor. One year later, on December 10, at his magnificent villa in San Remo on the Italian Riviera, Alfred Nobel died, and his remains were cremated.

When his will was read, a dynamite reaction followed. His nieces and nephews immediately contested it; Swedish King Oscar II was infuriated that the recipients were not merely limited to Swedes. Because Nobel had residences in several countries, each one laid claim to the will for its own tax purposes. Had it not been for Nobel's executor, Ragnar Sohlman, the will might have been declared null and void. Sohlman now faced the most difficult and dangerous job that any will executor ever had: to deliver Alfred's assets to the Swedish consulate in France before the Nobel family could stake its claim. He literally sat on millions of dollars, armed with a revolver, as he rode a horse-drawn cab through the streets of Paris.

After a three-year dispute, on December 10, the anniversary of Alfred's death, the first prizes could finally be distributed, in accordance with Nobel's final wishes. What would have brought the inventor infinite satisfaction was when, in 1896, Bertha von Suttner won the Nobel Prize for Peace. The award became, as a newspaper was to describe it, "the gold standard against which all other awards are measured."

Alfred Nobel was a man who had embodied many paradoxes: He was brilliant yet always felt inadequate; he was an advocate of peace and yet had invented an instrument of war; he was a patriot, but had mostly lived outside his native country. He had understood this aspect of his personality, as presaged with his words, "You say I am a riddle—it may be, for all of us are riddles unexplained."

Because of a eureka moment inspired by an erroneous obituary, Alfred Nobel had ensured that his legacy would not be as the "Merchant of Death," and "that the good would not be interred with his bones."

- The highlight of the Nobel Prize Award Ceremony in Stockholm is when the Nobel Laureate steps forward to receive the prize from the hands of the king of Sweden. The prizes are given to the laureates on December 10, the anniversary of Nobel's death.
- Boris Pasternak was awarded the Nobel Prize in 1958 for his novel *Dr. Zhivago*. Two days later, he sent the following tele-

gram to the Swedish Academy: "Immensely thankful, touched, proud, astonished, abashed." However, four days later, he sent another telegram: "Considering the meaning the Award has been given in the society to which I belong, I must refuse it. Please do not take offense at my voluntary rejection." Stalin had said that if Pasternak left to receive the award, he would be stripped of his Soviet citizenship and would not be allowed to return to Russia. Because Pasternak's lover, Olga, had to stay in the country, he was compelled to reject the award.

- Mahatma Gandhi was nominated for the Nobel Peace Prize five times but never received it
- Because of World War II, no prizes were awarded between the years 1940 and 1942. Hitler had issued a decree that forbade Germans from accepting Nobel Prizes.
- The Nobel Prize medals feature an image of Alfred Nobel in left profile.
- As part of his divorce settlement, Einstein's Nobel Prize went to his ex-wife, Mileva Maric.
- The first Nobel Prize Laureates collected 150,800 Swedish kroner (approximately $15,420 today). Currently the award is $1.5 million.

Eureka #8
(1895)

I n Lourdes, France, and in revival tents in the South, those who were blind claimed to be able to see, and those who were crippled claimed to be able to walk. However, because of a eureka moment, a man without faith was healed, with the result that "the laying on of hands" acquired a whole new meaning.

Daniel David (D.D.) Palmer, the man who was to give the adherents of Hippocrates a rival, was born a few miles outside of Toronto. When he was twenty, he and his older brother, with a tiny cash reserve, made their way on foot to the United States, a journey that took thirty days. He spent the years following the Civil War teaching school, raising bees, selling raspberries, and operating a grocery store in towns along the Mississippi River.

Palmer eventually moved to Iowa, where he married Abba Lord. This union ended after two years, then he wed Louvenia Landers and had four children. After her death, he married

Lavinia McGee; Martha Henning became the fourth Mrs. Palmer.

After two decades engaged in several different careers, he turned his attention to natural medicine, and within four years, his magnetic healing practice had made him extremely wealthy. From the onset of his practice, he believed there was one underlying cause of disease, and he was bent on discovering what he termed "the great secret." During these years, for reasons unknown, his latest wife was out of the picture, and he ended up with another spouse, Villa Amanda Thomas. Perhaps the fifth time proved to be the charm because it was during their marriage that he had his historic breakthrough.

On September 18, 1895, Palmer was working late at his office when he noticed a janitor, Harvey Lillard, cleaning. When a fire engine screeched by, Palmer was surprised to note that Harvey did not look up at the racket ensuing outside the window. He approached the janitor and struck up a conversation. He soon realized that it was fruitless, as the man was practically deaf. Palmer managed to communicate with Lillard, who could read lips, and discovered that Harvey had possessed normal hearing for most of his life. However, one day, when he had stood up from a cramped, stooping position, he had felt something "pop" in his back. For the past seventeen years, he had been enveloped in a world of silence. Palmer deduced that the popping in the back and the deafness had to be connected. Harvey gave permission for Palmer to run his hand down Lillard's spine; when he did so, he felt one of Harvey's vertebrae out of its normal position.

It was then that Palmer had his eureka moment: He determined that there was a correlation between the spine and other afflictions, and if a vertebra was adjusted, the other affliction would likewise be cured. After half an hour, Palmer convinced a reluctant Harvey to lie down on a bench. Palmer laid his hands on the janitor's spine and pushed the misaligned vertebra back into position. Overcome with emotion, Harvey expressed his amazement that he was now able to hear the wheels of the horse-drawn carts in the street below. A new branch of medicine had been born.

Palmer was eager to see if his theory of spinal adjustment would work a second time, and when it was successful with a patient experiencing heart trouble, he shelved his magnetic healing for this new form of practice. He felt that he had successfully unlocked "the great secret." Palmer asked his friend the Reverend Samuel Weed to help him christen his discovery. Weed suggested combining the Greek words *cheiros* and *praktikos* (meaning "done by hand") to describe the revolutionary treatment, thereby coining the term "chiropractic."

Palmer initially wanted to keep the new art of healing a family secret; however, the following year he opened a school offering a three-month program to teach the new practice. It would become known as the Palmer School of Cure, now known as the Palmer School of Chiropractic.

The established medical community was not thrilled with the man with his upstart methods, and they, along with the press, branded him a charlatan. Palmer was indicted for practicing medicine without a license and was sentenced to 105 days in jail; however, it stipulated he could be released earlier if he paid a fine of $350. After twenty-three days, Palmer capitulated and was released.

A further nightmare during this time was the death of

Villa from a morphine overdose. The following year, at age sixty, Palmer walked down the aisle with his sixth wife, Mary Hudler. The next day he became a grandfather when his son Bartlett Joshua (B.J.) gave birth to a son, also named Daniel David Palmer.

Embittered by his persecution, Palmer sold his practice to his son shortly after his release and moved to the West Coast, where he helped found chiropractor schools in Oklahoma, California, and Oregon. After the sale, the relationship between father and son became extremely bitter, to such an extent that Palmer stipulated in his will that his son was to be barred from attending his funeral.

In 1913, a final bizarre episode occurred in the tale of Palmer's life, when he was invited to attend a founder's day parade in Davenport in 1913 to celebrate the birth of chiropractic. While he was marching, he was struck from behind by B.J. Palmer, who had been the first person in Iowa to own a car. The courts eventually ruled it an accident, and no charges were laid. Several months later, in Los Angeles, D.D. Palmer passed away after a bout of typhoid fever. His ashes were placed in an urn and mounted in the large bust of his image in the Palmer School of Chiropractic.

For many decades, the established medical community refused to welcome to its fold this fledgling branch of healing. They thought of it as a practice of trick-or-treating; its practitioners, medicine men or witch doctors. In the 1960s, the American Medical Association condemned it as an unscientific cult.

After a twelve-year battle by the traditional doctors to have the upstart branch, whose adherents they referred to as "quackopractors," declared illegal, chiropractic was established as a medical science in 1983. Currently the field has 60,000 doctors. Thousands of people suffering from back pain enter their chiropractors' offices annually, only to reemerge, post adjustment, pain-free. For that they can thank a nineteenth-century magnetic healer whose eureka led to a laying on of healing hands.

- B.J. Palmer coined the radio term "broadcasting." He had the first radio station west of the Mississippi, WOC (Wonders of Chiropractic), and later WHO (With Hands Only).
- B.J. Palmer's wife, Mabel, became the first female chiropractor. Their son followed in their profession.

Eureka #9
(1899)

I n the nineteenth century, there were two brothers whose bond was as close as the biblical ones were contentious. And, because of a eureka, they made the world a far greater and, paradoxically, a far smaller place.

One simple toy seems to have made a great impact on humankind. In 1878, Midwestern minister Milton Wright brought home a surprise for sons Orville and Wilbur. Before the children could guess what it was, he released the flying toy into the air. The object left a lifelong impression. They named it "the Bat," and when it became dysfunctional from overuse, the mechanically adept duo built numerous copies.

After graduation from Dayton Central High School, the brothers eschewed college for life's classroom and deliberated their future. All they knew was that they wanted it to include an enterprise in which they could work together.

Their first undertaking was publishing a paper, the *West Side News*. One of the contributors was the only African American from their school, Paul Dunbar, the son of freed slaves. He, along with the brothers, was to achieve acclaim, but in a different venue. Dunbar became the first nationally known black poet; his most poignant lyric: "I know why the caged bird sings." When their newspaper folded, the brothers decided to capitalize on the bicycle craze consuming the nation and opened a shop. However, what distinguished it from the hundreds of other turn-of-the-century stores was that it doubled as a laboratory, where the owners produced wings and wheels.

At this time, the Wrights renewed their childhood interest, born from "the Bat," when they read newspapers about a German engineer named Otto Lilienthal, who had strapped a glider to his back and run down a hill until he was borne aloft. The brothers were intrigued with "the Flying Man." He was at the height of his fame when he plunged fifty feet, which crushed his spine. He died the next day in a Berlin hospital. His last words were, "Sacrifices must be made."

Wilbur wrote the Smithsonian requesting materials on flight; however, their true source of knowledge came from observing buzzards soaring above the skies of Dayton. It occurred to the brothers that birds balance themselves by adjusting the angle at which their wings meet the oncoming air. However, they pondered, man could not emulate this because an aircraft's wings, by their very nature, had to be rigid. That was, in Hamlet's words, the rub.

One day, while in his shop chatting with a customer, Wilbur absently started twisting a tube in opposite directions. Looking down at his hands, he had his eureka moment: A spiral twist running along an aircraft's wings would make the impossible possible—he had unlocked the secret of flight.

Ecstatic, Wilbur shared his eureka with Orville, and the two decided to waste no time in testing their theory. Armed with their revelation, they changed their belief from *if* man could fly to *when*. They decided to build a glider and test it in a place where there were strong steady winds, plenty of open space, and privacy. The site that met these three specifications was a remote fishing village in North Carolina called Kitty Hawk. The brothers erected a tent filled with their necessary supplies; in addition, Orville had his mandolin, Wilbur, his harmonica.

On December 17, 1903, after many experiments, the Wright brothers were ready for another test. Dressed in their customary dark suits and starched collars, they strode to their latest aircraft, which they had dubbed "the Flyer." In attendance were seven men who made up the crew of the Kill Devil Hills Lifesaving Station. The final step was to flip a coin to see which of them would man the flight. Orville called heads, which was the side that landed.

One of the onlookers, John Daniels, had set up a camera in case something miraculous took place. The ensuing image captured one of the most pivotal moments in history. The Flyer managed to stay airborne for twelve seconds; it covered a distance of 120 feet. In one brief moment, in a desolate outpost, the world changed forever.

Wilbur manned the next flight; he was airborne for fifty-nine seconds and covered 852 feet. However, when it was on the ground, a gust of wind caught the underside of a wing, and it started to rise into the air. Daniels yelled and dove toward what was arguably one of the greatest inventions of all time, hoping to pluck it back to earth. As he grabbed it, machine and man tumbled down the beach. In a matter of minutes, the world's first airplane was reduced to little more than driftwood on the shoreline. When Daniels was pulled from the carnage, he was unharmed. For the remainder of his days his greatest joy was to regale listeners with the tale of how he had survived the first plane crash.

Three months earlier, while seeing his sons off at the Dayton train station, Bishop Milton Wright had given Wilbur and Orville a dollar to cover the cost of a telegram as soon as the Flyer defied gravity. The brothers walked four miles up the beach to the Weather Bureau station at Kitty Hawk and sent a wire to their father. They were eager to share the celebration of their contemporary flying carpet. In the future, an eighty-two-year-old Bishop Wright ventured on a seven-minute flight, the first and only one in his life. During it, he was so exhilarated he exclaimed, "Higher, Orville, higher!" According to Milton's wishes, his sons never flew together except on one occasion, which they did with his permission. His decision was based on the terror of a double tragedy.

In 1908, the Department of War purchased a plane from the brothers for $25,000, and then the brothers turned their attention overseas. French newspapers were skeptical, and a popular question there was, "Are the Wrights fliers or liars?" Orville remained in the United States to work with the military, in the hopes his brainchild would prove a key to lasting peace. Wilbur headed for Le Mans, France, to put to rest the French belief that the Wrights had a "phantom machine." In France, the assembled crowd was awestruck with the miracle they witnessed, and the retiring pilot soon found himself in the role of international celebrity. Soldiers had to keep him from the crush of people who wanted to see him and the Flyer at close range.

On his end, Orville was wowing the masses on the other side of the Atlantic. However, one flight with a passenger, Lieutenant Thomas Selfridge, ended in a crash, which resulted in Selfridge's death. However, the brothers decided to shoulder on: "Sacrifices had to be made."

The Wright brothers were invited to the White House by President Taft and were equally venerated by European royalty; the German crown prince, Friedrich Wilhelm, in a burst of enthusiasm, took his jewel-encrusted stickpin from his necktie and gave it to the brothers. He said its diamond "W" had once stood for Wilhelm; now it was for Wright. When they returned to the United States, Wilbur flew across New York Harbor and circled the Statue of Liberty while a million awestruck New Yorkers looked on.

The brothers continued to live in the same home; they were lifelong bachelors and never had children. Wilbur once quipped that he "could not support a wife and a flying machine."

In 1912, Wilbur died from typhoid fever, tragic news that was covered on front pages the world over. Devastated, Orville was plunged into depression. He spent endless hours in his home, now a mansion, figuratively situated east of Eden, making replicas of the Bat for his grandnephews. Unlike Cain and Abel, the Wright brothers had delighted in nothing more than the unshakable bond between them; together they had conquered what had once only been the dominion of birds.

Orville died of a heart attack in 1948. Twenty-one years later, when Neil Armstrong landed on the moon, he carried with him a piece of the original cotton wing covering from the Wright Flyer. Because of a eureka in a bicycle shop in the Midwest, the Age of Flight was born. Man no longer had to be a caged bird, merely dreaming of freedom.

- Madame Hart O. Berg was the first female passenger; she flew with Wilber. Because in the Victorian era it was improper for a woman to show her ankles, her husband tied a cord around the bottom of her skirt before the flight. After she landed, she took a few hobbling steps before the cord was removed. That summer, the hobble skirt became the height of fashion.
- The Wright cycle shop and the Wright family home were purchased by Henry Ford.
- Only five bicycles built by the Wright brothers are still in existence.

Eureka #10

(1902)

Certain phrases are inexplicably associated with particular trials: Jesus Christ's trial with Pontius Pilate's words, "I wash my hands of the whole affair"; Susan B. Anthony's trial with her words, "Resistance to tyranny is obedience to God"; and O.J. Simpson's trial with Johnny Cochran's words, "If it doesn't fit, you must acquit." Similarly, in France there was a trial, and the quotation associated with it righted a terrible wrong. It also resulted in a eureka moment that provided the springboard from which a time-honored annual tradition was launched.

In 1894, Alfred Dreyfus, a young officer, was arrested for treason—namely, for leaking military information to the Germans. He was immediately suspected, mainly because he was the only Jewish person serving in the army. He had to undergo public humiliation: His rank marks and buttons were ripped off his uniform, and his saber was broken. He was sentenced to solitary confinement for life in the dreaded penal colony Devil's Island.

The famous French writer Emile Zola was enraged at the aberration of justice, in which the highest levels of government had been involved in a cover-up in order to secure Dreyfus' anti-Semitic conviction. He put France's justice system itself on trial in the public arena by writing a four-thousand-word letter with the rousing opening: *J'accuse!* ("I accuse!")

In the late nineteenth century, there was a newspaper, mainly dedicated to sports, called *Le Velo*; however, it also reported on current events and had corresponding political commentaries. Its editor, Pierre Giffard, was a staunch supporter of Alfred Dreyfus. Because of this, a conflict arose between him and his principal advertiser, the Count de Dion, who was satisfied with the outcome of the Dreyfus affair. Aware it would alienate his chief sponsor but committed to his belief that justice was more important than money, Giffard published the entire text of Zola's letter on the front page of *Le Velo*, with its glaringly controversial headline *"J'accuse!"*

Infuriated, the advertiser not only withdrew his business but also began his own rival sports newspaper, *L'Auto*, and hired Henri Desgrange as its editor. The upstart paper, printed on yellow sheets, was soon selling 25,000 copies, as many as its more established rival. After two years, the Count de Dion put pressure on his editor to surpass the sales of his detested rival. Because of this, Henri Desgrange called a company conference to think of a way to lure readers to *L'Auto*. When the editor asked if anyone had any ideas, the youngest man present (in the hope of gaining a raise from the parsimonious Desgrange), twenty-six-year-old Geo Lefevre, had his eureka moment: a six-day bicycle race around France. Desgrange replied, "As I understand it, petit Geo, you are suggesting a Tour de France."

The name had previously been used with regard to car racing; however, it was the first time it was used in reference to cycling. Intrigued, the older man took the younger one out for lunch, where the two continued to explore the novel idea. The site of the legendary meal, in the heart of Paris, was the Brasserie Zimmer, which later became the Brasserie Madrid and is now a T.G.I. Friday's.

The concept of a bicycle race was not new; however, it was the nature of the Tour de France that intrigued Desgrange. What Lefevre envisioned was a six-day race, over roads and through towns, that would involve several stages, rather than just on a traditional track. In this fashion, Lefevre explained, the race would come through the front yards of people's homes, which would intensify the thrill. The idea, mused the editor, might just be the publicity coup that would strike the more established newspaper, *Le Velo*, from its pedestal.

The editor still had grave doubts; namely, that the race would be one of utmost endurance and that no one would be up to such a grueling endeavor. However, because of both Lefevre's contagious enthusiasm and his promise to oversee all the details, Desgrange gave his grudging assent. He would arrange to advertise it on *L'Auto*'s yellow sheets, complete with a map of the proposed route. On November 20, 1902, the worldwide sporting phenomenon was born; the following year, the famous sporting event debuted.

To generate publicity for the race, a July 1, 1903, editorial in *L'Auto* read, "With the same sweeping, powerful gesture which Zola gave to his farm worker in La Terre, *L'Auto*, a newspaper of ideas and action, will launch across France, from today, those unknowing and forceful sowers of energy, the great professional road racing cyclists."

The 1903 event was a six-city, 1,509-mile race that would traverse Lyon, Marseille, Toulouse, Bordeaux, and Nantes, for which the sixty original participants, some of whom were circus performers and some of whom were jockeys, were paid 20,000 francs. They sported handlebar moustaches and bikes without gears; they encountered dirt roads and natural as well as man-made obstacles. Onlookers resorted to cheating for their friends or favorites to win: They placed nails and broken glass on the roads or formed human blockades. The competitors themselves often resorted to "the means justify the ends" in order to cross the finish line first. Between stages of the course, the riders would drink champagne or puff on cigarettes. They were known as the "convicts of the road." However, they were driven by the spirit of brawn, brains, and ambition that still pervades their modern-day counterparts.

Of the initial sixty contestants, twenty-one made it to the end. The winner of that inaugural Tour de France was Maurice Garin, who still holds the record for a win by the greatest margin of two hours and forty-nine minutes. He had persevered in a contest that had lasted three weeks and covered 2,175 miles, some of them over rugged mountain terrain. In a later account of his victory, he wrote, "With this race you (Desgrange) have revolutionized the Tour de France which will be a key date in the history of road racing." When more than 20,000 spectators lined up to see Garin, caked in mud and sweat, cross the finish line in Paris, it was apparent that Petit Geo was indeed deserving of that elusive raise.

The first Tour de France was a resounding success, and *L'Auto*'s sales skyrocketed. Its circulation jumped to 65,000, and by the 1923 tour, it was selling at the rate of 500,000 copies a day. It became the premier cycling newspaper. *L'Velo* could no longer compete, and within a year it folded. Giffard had paid a steep price for putting his principles over his pocketbook. Ironically, when Giffard passed away in 1923, Desgrange paid him a stirring tribute in *L'Auto*'s signature yellow-colored paper.

The Tour de France grew from its inception as a publicity stunt to the world's third-largest sporting event, after the Olympic Games and the World Cup. In 2002, it was estimated that 15 million French citizens flocked to the sides of the tour's roads, some having camped out a week ahead of time to procure the best view. More than 160 million viewers watch the participants vie to claim the yellow shirt, a tradition started by Desgrange so that the spectators would be able to determine from afar the contestant who was in the lead. He chose the color because of its clarity and because it matched the color of the pages of *L'Auto*.

When Henri Desgrange and Geo Lefevre sat in the Montmartre café and thought of a plan to outstrip their rival newspaper, they never in their wildest dreams imagined that their brainchild would morph into their country's most beloved sport, one which captures the attention of the world. Even more bizarrely, the Tour de France owes its origin to the rallying cry of denunciation, Emile Zola's *"J'accuse!"*

- Since its inception in 1903, the Tour de France has been an annual event with the exception of the years during the two world wars.

- Since 1975, the finish of the tour has been on the Champs-Elysées in Paris, the only time the avenue is closed other than for the processions of Bastille Day and for the Paris Marathon.
- A highly recognizable spectator who lines the roads to watch the tour is Didi Senft, who, in a red devil costume, has been known as El Diablo since 1993.

Eureka #11

(1912)

As a result of her eureka moment, a New York City woman took umbrage against an Old Testament injunction, which led to imprisonment and notoriety. However, she was willing to undergo privations and derision because she believed, with all her soul, that the path she trod was the one of righteousness.

Growing up in an Irish Catholic household, Margaret Louise Higgins was greatly influenced by her free-thinking father, whose occupation was chiseling stone angels on tombstones. She was also molded by her devoutly religious mother, who had been pregnant eighteen times. Determined to break out of her family's grim economic heritage (oftentimes her father forwent sculpting for drinking) and with financial assistance from two of her sisters, she enrolled in Claverack College. There she became active in theatrical groups and dreamed of becoming an actress. However, when she discovered she would have to divulge her leg measurements to get an acting job, she "turned to other fields where something besides legs was to count."

When Margaret's mother died from weakened health brought on by multiple childbearing and tuberculosis, Margaret decided on her occupation and enrolled in the nursing program at White Plains Hospital. In 1902, she married an architect, William Sanger, with whom she had three children. Several years later, the family relocated to New York City, where they became immersed in the pre-war, bohemian culture flourishing in Greenwich Village. They joined a circle that included intellectuals, activists, and artists, such as Upton Sinclair and Emma Goldman. Under their influence, she wrote a column for *The Call*, a socialist newspaper, titled "What Every Girl Should Know," which was on the radical topic of sex education.

This provided the first encounter in Margaret's lifelong battle with censors, who suppressed her column because it dealt with topics they deemed obscene, such as venereal disease. Enraged at the gag order, which violated the First Amendment, *The Call* ran an empty box under the caption "What Every Girl Should Know—Nothing, by Order of the United States Post Office!"

Along with her writing, Margaret worked in the Lower East Side slums of Manhattan, and it was in those tenements where she had the eureka moment that would later change the lives of women.

Margaret empathized with the plight of the women in the poverty-stricken neighborhoods because of her mother's life. The Book of Genesis exhorts the descendants of Adam and Eve "to be fruitful and multiply," but working in the tenements, Margaret realized the only result of being fruitful and multiplying seemed to be prematurely worn-out mothers and inadequately cared for children. Neighborhood women would crowd around Margaret, pleading, "Tell me something to keep me from having another baby. We cannot afford another yet."

In an era when buying a single condom made a person a criminal in thirty states, and priests told female parishioners that, if they prevented conception, they would be forever haunted by the faces of their unborn children, friends bandied about homespun remedies for unwanted pregnancies, including ingesting herb teas or turpentine, rolling down stairs, and inserting knitting needles. As a nurse, Margaret lamented that these old wives' tales could not be shattered by scientific information.

On a stifling July day in 1912, Margaret received a call from a distraught husband, Jake Sachs, to assist his Russian Jewish wife, Sadie, who was suffering the effects of trying to terminate her fourth pregnancy. As the doctor was leaving, Sadie begged him to help prevent another conception. His response was she couldn't have her cake and eat it, too. Then he added, in a stab at humor, "Tell Jake to sleep on the roof." Margaret felt despair that she was unable to help those who were in dire need of assistance.

Three months later, Margaret was summoned to assist Sadie once more, again with the same affliction. This time, however, Sadie was already in a coma and died not more than ten minutes later. As Margaret folded the dead woman's arms, she had her eureka moment: She determined her life's mission would be to assist women in taking control of their own bodies, thereby ending "miseries which were as vast as the sky."

She was to become a self-appointed evangelist, her pulpit, that sex could be separated from procreation. She was prepared to step into the boxing ring, knowing full well her opponents would be powerful ones: the Catholic Church, the American government, and public opinion.

Margaret gave up nursing to embark on a crusade to limit family size. She began writing a monthly magazine, *The Woman Rebel*, in which she passionately urged for what was then called "voluntary motherhood," and wherein she coined the term "birth control." Its slogan was "No Gods and No Masters." Although the movies of the era were silent, Ms. Sanger was not. After only six issues, she was arrested and indicted for distributing "obscene" literature through the mail. She was charged with nine counts of violating obscenity laws, which carried a maximum sentence of forty-five years in prison. Margaret fled to London, where she practiced her philosophy that each woman be "the absolute mistress of her own body" and had affairs with the high-profile psychologist Havelock Ellis and the novelist H. G. Wells. While she was gone, her husband, William, gave out his wife's magazine to a woman who said she was in need of birth control. In reality, she was working for the police, and he was sentenced to a month behind bars. The combination of his incarceration, Margaret's two-year absence, and her marital infidelities led to their divorce. Margaret later married wealthy oil magnate Noah H. Slee, who agreed to both accept her sexual liaisons and finance her birth control movement. Margaret kept her first husband's then-famous (or infamous) last name.

In 1916, Margaret Sanger returned to the United States and soon lost her five-year-old daughter, Peggy, to pneumonia. Partially in sympathy, the charges against her were dropped.

The crusader and her sister then began to push their ideas in earnest. Although women could not vote, Margaret hoped females could at least control propagation. Sanger and her sister set up America's first contraceptive clinic in Browns-ville, Brooklyn, which later adopted the name Planned Parenthood. Hundreds of women lined up for blocks. Apparently the men of New York were not keen on sleeping on the roof.

Nine days later, there was a raid. One woman chased the police car, shouting, "Come back! Come back and save me!" The birth control sisters were sent to the workhouse for creating a public nuisance. Margaret said of the efforts to silence her, "I see immense advantages in being gagged. It silences me but it makes millions of others talk about me and the cause in which I live."

Margaret Sanger remained a rebel dedicated to her cause. When the Pill was finally approved in 1960, Sanger was an eighty-year-old widow living in a Tucson nursing home. She celebrated the news by uncorking a bottle of champagne and sipping it alone.

Because of a eureka brought on by a death in a slum tenement, a movement was launched for women's reproductive freedom. To Margaret Sanger's detractors, she was a female Satan; to her supporters, she was what her father had once carved to grace tombstones: a stone angel.

- In 1965, a few months prior to Sanger's death, the Supreme Court decision *Griswold v. Connecticut* made birth control legal for married couples.

- In 1921, Sanger started the magazine *The Birth Control Review*. In response, she received more than 1 million letters from women throughout the country. A common concern from women was that they couldn't get an education or decent job because of the endless cycle of pregnancy. Sanger felt that if the legislators read the letters, they would be empathic to women's plight, and accordingly, Sanger compiled five hundred of the letters into a book, *Mothers in Bondage*.

- In 1925, Sanger gave a lecture on birth control to the women's auxiliary of the Ku Klux Klan in Silver Lake, New Jersey.

- Sanger helped fund research that led to Gregory Pincus' development of the birth control pill.

Eureka #12
(1918)

Shakespeare's view of humor was "brevity is the soul of wit." Dorothy Parker's view of erotic apparel was "brevity is the soul of lingerie." And Frank Lloyd Wright's view of architecture was "less is more." One Midwesterner also concurred with a philosophy of conciseness, which led to a eureka moment that made him, along with his trademark Pegasus, the king of Pleasantville.

William Roy DeWitt Wallace was born in Minnesota; his father, a Presbyterian preacher and Greek scholar, was the president of Macalester College. With five children and a modest salary, Dr. Wallace raised his family in the stern fashion of his own boyhood, on a diet of cornmeal mush and endless prayer.

Growing up, DeWitt rebelled against his father's values and tried to prove he was not the stereotypical son of a minister, instead becoming known as an indifferent student who loved pranks. When a cow was discovered in the third-floor chapel, all fingers pointed to DeWitt.

He attended Macalester for two years; after his sophomore year, he transferred to the University of California at Berkeley. There he enrolled again as a freshman because, as he explained, "The freshman year is more fun."

During a Christmas vacation, a friend from Macalester, Barclay Acheson, took Wallace home with him to Washington. DeWitt was taken with Barclay's sister, Lila Bell, but she was, he sadly learned, already engaged.

The following year, DeWitt dropped out of college and returned to St. Paul, where he had a job writing for a farm-book publisher. He was barely eking out a living when, while lying on a hayfield in Montana, he had the idea to create his own book, a compilation of all the free pamphlets on farming, so readers could get the pertinent information from a single source. Acting on his hunch, DeWitt quit his job, condensed the material, and hitchhiked through the West, selling his condensed books to banks and feed stores, who gave them as gifts to customers. He barely broke even and abandoned the business when he enlisted in World War I.

In France, he was hit by four pieces of shrapnel and had to spend four months in a military hospital. To while away the endless hours, the young sergeant devoured American magazines. His main criticism was that although the articles were on interesting subjects, they were too lengthy. For diversion, he did what he had done back home with his farm manuals.

When he returned to St. Paul, unemployed and a college dropout, DeWitt was facing a bleak future. He then recalled what had intrigued him when he had lain on a hayfield in Montana and when he had lain in his hospital bed in France. These reminiscences led to his eureka moment: He decided he would make a magazine by condensing long articles into concise ones. He realized Americans were busy people and yet wanted to keep abreast of the latest information. His work would be a compilation of the leading periodicals of the day, thereby satisfying people's quest for knowledge in bite-size portions. They would be pertinent yet not mentally exerting, something to be digested over coffee and discussed at the water cooler.

For the next six months, DeWitt's home away from home was the periodical room of the Minneapolis Public Library. DeWitt's formula was highbrow for the lowbrow. Its overall tone was one of optimism; although his pamphlet did address the world's problems, the overall message was that with God's help, America would forever prevail. In the digest world, faith can indeed move mountains, and readers are left with a warm feeling about themselves, about life, and about the pocket-size magazine.

DeWitt was filled with enthusiasm for his brainchild and sent out copies to the leading Manhattan editors, with the hope they would fund his venture and hire him as an editor. The response was met with utter indifference. They scoffed at the idea of a magazine consisting of condensed versions from other magazines. The only encouraging response was from William Randolph Hearst, who thought such a periodical might attain a circulation of 300,000, which was too minimal for his publishing empire.

At this time DeWitt ran into his old school friend Barclay Acheson, who had become a Presbyterian minister. When DeWitt asked about his sister, Lila Bell, he was informed that her engagement had fallen through, and that during the war she had devoted herself to volunteering by helping women factory workers, and was still engaged in that pursuit. DeWitt sent Lila Bell a telegram: "Conditions Among Women Workers in St. Paul Ghastly Stop Urge Immediate Investigation." Coincidentally, a week later she was temporarily assigned to work in St. Paul, and DeWitt and Lila Bell met again for the first time in eight years. Bashfully, he showed her the cover of his rejected magazine. Her response was, "It was a gorgeous idea." On the first night, DeWitt proposed; on the second, she accepted. They were married in Pleasantville, New York, in 1921.

The next step was for the couple to turn "the gorgeous idea" into a reality. They borrowed $4,000 from the Wallace family to launch their dream. They sent out five thousand copies of their *Reader's Digest*, vol. 1, no. 1. Its logo was a black Pegasus, chosen by Lila, because she said according to myth, when Pegasus stamps his feet, writers receive inspiration. The logo was to remain in place until 2007. The copies were mailed out from their office, a rented basement room under a Greenwich Village speakeasy. Then they left on a two-week honeymoon to the Poconos. When they returned, they were greeted with fifteen hundred orders, each containing the annual subscription of $3. Later Lila recalled, "I was enthralled that so many had answered. He was disappointed because everybody hadn't."

When the debut issue of five thousand copies arrived from the Pittsburgh printer, DeWitt hired the barflies from the speakeasy to help him and Lila wrap and address them. Then they piled the mail sacks into a taxicab and took them to the post office. When they finished, they stopped in a café to toast the future.

The magazine, with its Norman Rockwell view of America, was half the size of other magazines, which later led to its slogan "America in your pocket." It quickly became a veritable "little engine that could." The Wallaces added the classic feature "Most Unforgettable Character" (where readers could interactively submit their own stories). Editions carried inspiring stories of everyday Americans who made it against all odds. *Time* magazine, in a 1951 article called "The Common Touch," wrote, "It is read in foxholes in Korea, in the cockpits of transatlantic planes, by Swedish farmers, Brazilian housewives, Japanese coal miners, Igorots in G strings." Soon the Pleasantville post office was inundated.

As the coffers began to fill, the couple moved their office from its cramped basement to nearby Chappaqua, on eighty aces of farmland. The cost was $1.5 million, which was an astronomical amount in the 1930s. They built their headquarters in a colonial Williamsburg style, and its walls were adorned with French Impressionist paintings and the rooms filled with costly antiques. In individual offices, there were masterpieces by Renoir, Braque, and Chagall. The building also sported the magazine's logo: Four green, winged horses adorn its thirty-two-foot white cupola.

Despite the change of locale, the Wallaces kept the postal address of Pleasantville because of the positive association of the name. Similarly, with their newfound wealth, they purchased an estate, High Winds. The 105-acre estate, built on a bluff above a small lake five miles from the *Digest* headquarters, featured a five-bedroom structure that resembled a castle.

Because DeWitt was a shy man, with a Garboesque aversion to publicity, the couple had little social life outside of a few business-related affairs. Evenings often found Lila in DeWitt's arms, where, after dinner, they danced for fifteen minutes in their rumpus room. However, when social duty called, DeWitt answered. He constructed the guesthouse where the Wallaces would host lavish parties, whose guests included Presidents Ronald Reagan and Gerald Ford, Reverend Billy Graham, Mayor Ed Koch, Dan Rather, Alex Haley, Dave Thomas, and John Walsh.

The couple, who remained childless, became the country's foremost philanthropists. As their personal fortune increased, Lila Bell devoted less time at the helm of *Reader's Digest* and more time in philanthropic pursuits. She donated $60 million to her favorite charities and numerous Presbyterian causes. She also undertook the restoration of Monet's house and garden at Giverny. DeWitt's maxim was "The dead carry with them to the grave in their clutched hands only that which they have given away." For their work, they were both awarded the Presidential Medal of Freedom.

William Roy DeWitt Wallace, the originator of the simple formula, was himself a complex man; indeed, he was the prototype of the Most Unforgettable Character. On the one hand, he retained vestiges of the teenage prankster; for example, he learned to fly his own plane and enjoyed scaring Lila by buzzing their home. On the other hand, he was a chronic worrier, torn by inner doubts and subject to bouts of deep melancholy. Though he was devoted to Lila Bell, whom he praised as "that incredible and slavish woman," he was also a womanizer. DeWitt's greatest indiscretion was an affair with Lila's favorite niece, Judy, who, with her husband, Fred Thompson, had been heirs to the empire—that is, until the cat slipped out of its bag. Unable to perform a beheading, Lila settled on disinheritance.

When DeWitt Wallace passed away, his magazine had mushroomed into a multibillion-dollar empire, leaving behind a success story that could have been lifted from the very pages of his own eureka-inspired magazine, *Reader's Digest.*

- *Reader's Digest* accounts for approximately 666 million pieces of mail that pass through the Pleasantville post office each year.
- In 2007, the Ripplewood Holdings acquired the magazine for $1.6 billion.
- John Heidenry wrote a biography of the Wallaces, *Theirs Was the Kingdom.*

Eureka #13
(1923)

In the early years of the twentieth century, there was one eureka moment that led to another, both of which impacted the face of America. However, the former was in tribute to men many people would rather not remember; the latter, to men many people would rather not forget.

In 1909, Caroline Helen Jemison Plane, a chapter president of the United Daughters of the Confederacy, gazed at Stone Mountain in Georgia and had a eureka moment: She decided the mountain would be a perfect place to sculpt her hero, the Confederate General Robert E. Lee. Her organization enthusiastically agreed, and they hired renowned sculptor (John) Gutzon de la Mothe Borglum to depict a twenty-foot visage of the general. Not surprisingly, he told the United Daughters of the Confederacy that the scope of the project would have to be more far-reaching than what they had planned: "Ladies, a twenty-foot head of Lee in that mountain would look like a postage stamp on a barn door." Instead, he proposed three Confederate heroes—General Lee, Stonewall Jackson, and

President Jefferson Davis—riding across the mountain on horseback, clad in full military regalia, followed by a legion of artillery troops. However, with the advent of World War I, the plans were delayed until several years later.

In the interim, on a Thanksgiving evening in 1915, a group of men, inspired by D. W. Griffith's film *The Birth of a Nation*, gathered on Stone Mountain, attracted to the site because of its proposed Civil War memorial. William J. Simmons read a few verses from his Bible and then the group, clad in white robes, burned a cross. The ritual robes had originally been adopted by the Klan to terrorize the superstitious former slaves into believing that they were ghosts. An oath of fealty was read by Nathan B. Forrest II, the grandson of the original Imperial Grand Wizard, General Nathan B. Forrest, and the Ku Klux Klan, which had been in hibernation for half a century, was reborn. It was in allusion to this that Dr. Martin Luther King Jr., in his "I have a dream" speech, exhorted, "Let freedom ring from Stone Mountain of Georgia!"

After the war, carving of the monument resumed, and on January 19, 1924, the birthday of General Lee, thousands of spectators were on hand for the unveiling. Vice President Spiro Agnew dedicated the near-finished monument in 1970, filling in for President Nixon, who was embroiled in the Kent State tragedy. However, the final carving was not undertaken by Borglum, as his relationship with the United Daughters of the Confederacy and the Klan had broken down to such an extent that the sculptor fled Georgia to avoid arrest by the police and the fury of the white robed.

Because of the notoriety of Stone Mountain, newspapers across the country were not at a loss for stories. One man who read about Stone Mountain with more than a passing interest was Jonah LeRoy Robinson, the official historian for South Dakota. The story led to his eureka moment: to carve giant figures to increase tourism in his impoverished state. His dream, which he hoped would put Black Hills on the map, was to carve giant likenesses of Western figures such as Chief Red Cloud, Buffalo Bill Cody, Lewis and Clark, and legendary Sioux warriors marching along the skyline. Not only did he have the inspiration but he also had an artist in mind: master sculptor Gutzon Borglum.

When Borglum arrived, Robinson discovered that the artist had an ego the size of the mountain he was to sculpt. Immediately Borglum informed Robinson he was not going to waste his time immortalizing regional heroes. He insisted his work demanded a subject national in nature and explained that his vision consisted of carving four great presidential figures, whose visages would serve as a monument of the birth of democracy. He said, "A nation's memorial should, like Washington, Jefferson, Lincoln, and Roosevelt, have serenity, nobility, a power that reflects the gods who inspired them and suggests the gods they have become." Robinson concurred; for him to fight the narcissistic Borglum would have been akin to moving a mountain.

When Borglum climbed Mount Rushmore, via its Harney Peak, he knew that the spot, which was the highest point between the Rockies and the Swiss Alps, was going to be his canvas; its monument, his immortality. As he gazed out at the awe-inspiring vista, he stated, "Here is the place—American history shall march along that skyline."

However, Robinson and Borglum soon faced stony opposition. Environmentalists questioned how a mortal sculptor could hope to improve on an immortal work of art. Robinson would not be deterred. He responded, "God only makes a Michelangelo or a Gutzon Borglum once in a thousand years." The fiercest struggle, however, came from the Lakota Sioux.

In the treaty of 1868, the U.S. government had promised the Sioux nation the territory that included the Black Hills for perpetuity. However, "perpetuity" only lasted until gold was found, after which the Native Americans were forcibly evacuated. This fact was especially devastating because the land of the Black Hills was their sacred burial grounds. Therefore, the last thing the Sioux would want would be thousands of tourists trampling on their ancestors' graves to see monolithic visages of the men who had founded a way of life that had destroyed their own. However, the uproar soon died down, as most assumed the undertaking was merely an impossible dream.

As Borglum stood at the foot of his mountain, the task before him was a Herculean labor: His project was to create a modern-day Colossus of Rhodes without any guaranteed source of funding, backed mainly by a minor state official, amid hostility as great as he had faced in his last aborted project. Other men would have fled; Borglum had at last found the mistress he would embrace for the remainder of his days.

Despite the problems that beset his dream, Robinson continued to pursue his and Borglum's vision; the main concern was financing the mammoth undertaking. It was at this point that serendipity stepped in, in the guise of a humid Washington summer. In order to escape the heat, Calvin Coolidge had decided to vacation for three weeks in South Dakota. The need for funds coincided with the arrival of a president who was to look favorably on the carving of four of his predecessors.

The Mount Rushmore Committee leaped at the opportunity to garner his support. They changed the name of Hanging Squaw Creek to Grace Coolidge Creek, after the First Lady. They rigged the water with chicken wire and stocked it with trout from a nearby fish hatchery, so that the amateur angler would meet with success. They also scrambled to remodel the rustic State Game Lodge in Custer State Park until it was fit to be the president's summer White House.

On June 15, ten thousand South Dakotans were on hand to greet the First Couple, along with their two dogs and pet raccoon. Soon, in a good mood from his skill at fishing, Coolidge rode on horseback to Mount Rushmore, attired in cowboy boots and a ten-gallon hat, a present from the local residents. He allotted the money with the words, "We have come here to dedicate a cornerstone laid by the hand of the Almighty." His caveat was that besides Washington, two Republicans and one Democrat be portrayed.

Given the go-ahead, four hundred local workers labored for fourteen years; they dynamited and sculpted the granite into the image of four famous faces, at a cost of $989,992. Shortly before its completion, Gutzon Borglum died. His son, Lincoln, finished the hair and faces on the four gargantuan visages. Even then, the likenesses were not complete; the sculptor intentionally left three extra inches of granite on the surface so that nature, in the form of erosion, would finish carving Mount Rushmore over the next twenty thousand years, thereby making the divine play a hand in its creation.

Because of one eureka that led to another, a state historian and a modern-day Michelangelo left their imprint on the Black Hills, creating a landmark that would last in perpetuity.

- Alfred Hitchcock, for his 1959 movie *North by Northwest*, planned to film the chase scene on Mount Rushmore. He wanted Cary Grant to hide in Lincoln's nostril and then have a fit of sneezing. The Parks Commission of the Department of the Interior responded to the director's request by asking how he would like it if they had Lincoln play the scene in Cary Grant's nose. Hitchcock saw their point, and the scene was shot on a model of the monument at MGM studio.

- The monument's mountain was originally known to the Lakota Sioux as Six Grandfathers. It was renamed after Charles E. Rushmore, a prominent New York lawyer, during an expedition to the area in 1885. He had made the journey accompanied by David Swanzey, whose wife, Carrie, was the sister of author Laura Ingalls Wilder.

- In 1937, a bill was introduced in Congress to add the head of suffragette Susan B. Anthony; however, the feds prescribed that the funds only be used to finish the original project.

- Originally, the figures were to be carved from the waist up, but there weren't sufficient funds. Borglum had also planned a massive panel in the shape of the Louisiana Purchase, on top of which would have been, in eight-foot-tall gilded letters, the Declaration of Independence and the U.S. Constitution.

- In 2004, over 2 million visitors traveled to the memorial.

Eureka #14
(1926)

I n the furthermost reaches of our memories, and buried deep in our closets, are cherished mementos from our childhood: a doll, a tin soldier, a stuffed animal. It was to them we whispered our fears, our dreams. However, because of a eureka moment, one person felt his youthful companion was used against him, and it became a shadow that dogged his life's footsteps. However, although it brought grief to its namesake, it brought endless delight to millions.

Alan Alexander Milne attended a small school run by his father, where one of his teachers, H. G. Wells, would one day find acclaim as a writer. He attended Cambridge on a mathematics scholarship; postgraduation, he left for London to pursue his dream of a literary career, but the muse of inspiration proved elusive. In his autobiography, he wrote, "Ideas may drift into other minds, but they do not drift my way. I have to go and fetch them. I know no work manual or mental to equal the appalling heart-breaking anguish of fetching an idea from nowhere."

In London, Alan met Owen Seaman, the owner of *Punch*, who gave him a job and also introduced him to his goddaughter, Dorothy de Sélincourt, at her coming-out dance. Alan was endeared to her when she laughed at his jokes; the two married in 1913. During World War I, Alan joined the British Army and was sent home two nightmarish years later when he developed trench fever.

A year later, the couple had their only child. They had originally wanted to call him Billie, but concluding that it was too informal, they christened him Christopher. As a toddler, he mispronounced his surname, Milne, as Moon, and this earned him his nickname, Billie Moon. Dorothy's first birthday present for her toddler was an Alpha Farnell teddy bear from Harrod's, which was approximately two feet tall and light brown. The new owner called him Edward.

When Christopher was six, the Milnes moved to Cotchford, in East Sussex, on the outskirts of Ashwood Forest. Inspired by his son's evening prayers, Alan wrote a collection of poetry titled *Vespers*, intended only for his family. Dorothy, enchanted, sent it to *Vanity Fair* in New York. Alan laughed off her attempts, but told her she could keep any money it made. It turned out to be a very expensive present, as readers soon clamored for more.

Encouraged by its success, he soon started penning other works for children. One of his stories, "When We Were Young," became extremely popular with a generation eager to substitute the horrors of a world war with a tale of childhood innocence. Its dedication reads: "To Billie Moon."

Alan read to his son from the works of P. G. Wodehouse (one of his favorite authors) and also took him on visits to the

London Zoo. One of the exhibits they saw featured a Canadian bear called Winnipeg. As that was difficult to pronounce, Christopher shortened it to Winnie, the moniker he would later confer on his own stuffed animal, in place of Edward. (He added Pooh from a name he had given a swan that floated around the grounds of the family home.) Enraptured, Christopher begged his father to take the Canadian bear home. Milne was to comply with his son's request, though not in the manner Christopher had expected.

Other stuffed animals joined Christopher's collection: Piglet, Kanga, Roo, Tigger, and Eeyore. To entertain his son, Alan would make up stories about Winnie-the-Pooh, whom he called "the bear of very little brain." Of course, the hero of the stories was Christopher, and the backdrop for their adventures was nearby Ashdown Forest, forever immortalized as the Enchanted Place.

One evening, after yet another story involving Christopher's stuffed animals, Alan had his eureka moment: The tales he told his son could be the basis for a children's book. They became *Winnie-the-Pooh* and its sequel, *The House at Pooh Corner*; Alan, who used the pen name A. A. Milne, became one of the most beloved children's authors of all time.

Soon the family's quiet country retreat was the scene of a publicity storm, where photographers took pictures of the famous father, son, and bear. One of these, with Christopher holding his beloved stuffed animal, currently hangs in the London Gallery. Not too bad for "a bear of very little brain."

As it turned out, there were few detractors of *Winnie-the-Pooh*. One notable critic, however, was Dorothy Parker, who wrote her column for the *New Yorker* under the title Constant

Reader. Parker had panned *Now We Are Six* a year before her review of *The House at Pooh Corner*, though she had acknowledged that "to speak against Mr. Milne puts one immediately in the ranks of those who set fire to orphanages."

The House at Pooh Corner proved to be one pot of honey too many for the acerbic critic. The breaking point for Parker was when Pooh revealed that he added the "tiddely pom" to his Outdoor Song "to make it more hummy." Her caustic ink stated, "And it is that word 'hummy,' my darlings, that marks the first place in *The House at Pooh Corner* at which Tonstant Weader fwowed up." Parker did not have any personal malice against Milne. As she had written in her review of *Now We Are Six*, "Time was when A. A. Milne was my hero, but that when Mr. Milne went quaint, all was over. Now he leads his life, and I lead mine." Sadly, her relationship toward Alan was soon to be followed by his son's similar alienation.

The chasm between A. A. Milne and his son first began when Christopher was at boarding school. There, as the namesake of his famous fictional alter ego, he became the butt of his peers. Years earlier, a gramophone recording of Christopher singing the poem *Vespers* had been made, and to his horror, one of his classmates had a copy. Christopher would cringe when he heard his younger voice singing, "Hush! Hush! Whisper? Who dares? Christopher Robin is saying his prayers." In his autobiography, he wrote of this childhood horror, "I vividly recall how intensely painful it was to me to sit in my study at Stowe while my neighbors played the famous—and now cursed—gramophone record remorselessly over and over again. Eventually, the joke, if not the record, wore out, they handed it to me, and I took it and broke it into a hundred fragments and scattered them over a distant field."

He took up boxing as a way to defend himself against his tormentors. Christopher began to see *Winnie-the-Pooh* as an exploitation of his childhood, which had thrust him into this unwilling spotlight. In his publication *The Enchanted Places*, he wrote, "It seemed to me, almost, that my father had got to where he was by climbing upon my infant shoulders, that he had filched from me my good name and had left me with nothing but the empty fame of being his son."

The chasm between Christopher and his parents further widened when Christopher married his first cousin, Lesley de Sélincourt, the daughter of his mother's estranged brother Aubrey, whom Dorothy had not spoken to for thirty years. To distance him from his childhood home and its albatross legacy, Christopher and his wife left for Dartmouth.

In Dartmouth, as if in defiance of the damage the books had caused him, the couple started their own business, the Harbour Bookshop. Though he and Lesley loved running it, one source of frustration was when clients brought in their Winnie-mad progeny, so they could shake hands with the original Christopher Robin. Their only child, Claire, was born with a severe case of cerebral palsy. The Milne family had traveled far from the Hundred Acre Wood, where nothing so tragic ever happened that a pot of honey could not fix.

In October 1952, Alan suffered a stroke that incapacitated him for his remaining years. During this time, his son seldom returned home. He stuck to his conviction that his father's "heart remained buttoned up all through his life." Whether Milne did exploit his son for his own ends or whether his son misconstrued the situation as a scapegoat for his own life's disappointments must forever be relegated to that grayest of areas, the world of subjectivity.

The fictional Christopher once beseeched his beloved friend, "'Pooh, if I—if I'm not quite'—he stopped and tried again—'Pooh, whatever happens, you will understand, won't you?'" Perhaps just as Winnie always did understand, and forgive, Christopher, ultimately, was able to do likewise.

- Cotchford Farm was where the Rolling Stones' lead guitarist Brian Jones lived and where he drowned in 1969.
- Milne was a lifelong friend of the author of another children's classic—James Barrie, the author of *Peter Pan*.
- A street in Warsaw and another in Hungary is named after Winnie-the-Pooh.
- Pooh's official birth date is August 21, 1921, the day Christopher Robin received him as a present on his first birthday.
- Christopher's stuffed animals currently reside in state in a climate-controlled case in the New York Public Library.
- The Pooh books were favorites of Walt Disney's daughters, and they inspired Disney to bring Pooh to film in 1966. In 1993, the Walt Disney Company acknowledged that Pooh Bear is second only to Mickey Mouse in their portfolio of the most beloved Disney characters. He is also a moneymaker: Pooh merchandise brings in a billion dollars in annual revenue for Disney.

Eureka #15
(1927)

Wait a minute, wait a minute. You ain't heard nothin' yet, folks" were the first words spoken in the "talkie" film *The Jazz Singer*. In its earliest showing, the astounded audience leaped up and cheered; to one young man, it led to his eureka moment. The result of his brainstorm was an iconic four-fingered figure who would wield a scepter in the world of animation.

Elias Disney left Canada for the United States, seeking to make his fortune in the Gold Rush. He named his fourth son Walter Elias, after Walter Parr, the minister of his church. He settled in Chicago, but fearing the influences of a big city on his children, he later bought a farm in Marceline, Missouri.

As a child, Walter became attached to the numerous farm animals, which he endlessly sketched. Once he drew them in tar on the outside of his house; this artistic endeavor earned him a beating from his unimpressed father.

Unfortunately, the financial security Elias sought in the United States escaped him. Money became so scarce he instructed his wife to sell all the butter she churned. Unwilling to feed her children dry bread, and also not wanting to incur the wrath of her husband, she surreptitiously buttered her children's bread and instructed them to eat it butter-side down.

When Elias decided to try his elusive luck in Kansas, only three children made the move; the two older sons had taken off, unable to cohabit with Elias.

In the new state, Elias' job was to organize the delivery of the *Kansas City Star*. Walter and his brother Roy were assigned to rise at 3:30 a.m. to make sure customers received their newspapers on time. While the other boys received $3 a week, Elias refused to pay his sons, saying he paid them in food and clothing. In anger, Roy, like his two older brothers, left home.

Soon the family was on the move, back to Chicago. There Walter enrolled in the Chicago Institute of Art, over his father's protests that art would never put bread on the table. When he was sixteen, for escape and adventure Walter falsified his birth certificate and enlisted in World War I, serving in France as an ambulance driver. His vehicle was distinctive because of the fanciful drawings he painted on its exterior.

After returning from Europe, Walter decided to join Roy, who was working at a bank in Santa Monica. He arrived with $40 in the pocket of his well-worn jacket, a sketchpad, and an irrepressible imagination. He convinced his brother to go into business, and with Roy's $200 savings and some additional begged and borrowed funds, they started the Disney Bros. Studio. To look more like a studio boss, Walter grew a moustache; he also shortened his name to Walt.

The company also included Ub Iwerks, whom Disney had met in 1919 when they both worked for an art studio in Kansas, and Lillian Bond, who worked at the Disney studio in "ink and paint" of the cartoon cells. The former became Walt's lifelong collaborator; the latter became his lifelong wife. Taking time away from his sketchpad, Walt asked Lillian out on a first date to the Broadway show *No, No, Nanette*. This progressed to random drives in the hills of Los Angeles. On one of these drives he asked her if he should buy a new car for himself or a ring for her. She chose the ring.

Iwerks and Disney's chief creation was Oswald the Lucky Rabbit; however, its rights were owned by a New York City firm that ended up stealing Walt's idea and then firing him when he refused to give in to its financial machinations. He vowed to never cede artistic license to anyone ever again.

On the long train ride back to California from New York, Walt desperately needed inspiration, and it came to him in the form of what was to become the most famous rodent in history: a mouse. After showing his initial sketch to Lillian, she vetoed his suggested name of Mortimer as being too pretentious and suggested Mickey.

Back at his studio, Disney determined that animation was the best medium for his cartoon and set about making his one-dimensional creation into an animated one. Before Mickey's debut, serendipity stepped in. *The Jazz Singer*, the first film to employ sound, was released. This led to Walt's eureka moment: What would make Mickey stand out from other animated characters was the introduction of sound, something no other studio had attempted.

In *Steamboat Willie*, in which the famous rodent debuted,

Mickey's voice was Walt's own, and the mouse has not stopped talking since. Walt had an orchestra synchronized to the action, and the result proved a sensation when it premiered in Manhattan on November 18, 1928. The date would become the first birthday of Mickey Mouse. Soon a Mickey merchandising blitz ensued, and his trademark ears became ubiquitous.

Other famous animal figures followed, inspired by the ones from his childhood farm, making Walt a modern-day Aesop and, ultimately, a modern-day Midas. Speaking of the character who had become his alter ego, Disney stated, "When people laugh at Mickey Mouse, it's because he's so human; and that is the secret of his popularity. I only hope that we don't lose sight of one thing—that it was all started by a mouse."

Unfortunately, Disney's meteoric rise came with a personal price. He was such a workaholic that Lillian referred to herself as a mouse widow. His frenetic pace at the studio, chronic chain smoking, and rapid mood swings, coupled with the devastation of his wife's miscarriage, resulted in what he called "a hell of a breakdown." To recover his emotional equilibrium, Lillian and Walt took a Caribbean cruise.

In 1933, the couple was overjoyed with the birth of their daughter, Diane. Three years later, they adopted a girl named Sharon Mae. Although Walt was always faithful to his wife and a doting father to his daughters, he once stated, "I have loved Mickey Mouse more than any woman I have ever known."

Walt Disney's brainchild, Mickey, opened the floodgate as to what would become his niche, and a host of beloved films that would become a part of America's cultural literacy followed. In 1934, he embarked on his most daring project. This time, instead of an animated short that preceded the main feature, his new project would be one that would become a feature film, the first animated to do so. Furthermore, it was the first animation to employ color. The $2 million project was an astronomical sum in the midst of the Great Depression, and other studio heads referred to it as "Disney's Folly." It proved to be anything but. It premiered at the Cathay Theater in Los Angeles in 1937, and when it was over, the audience gave its subjects—Snow White and her faithful dwarves—a standing ovation. At the premiere, John Barrymore bounced up and down on his seat with excitement, while Clark Gable and Carol Lombard were spotted crying at the end. The film garnered revenues of $8 million (today $98 million). Walt Disney was rewarded at the Academy Awards with one regular-size Oscar and seven miniature ones. Disney's comment on his astounding achievements was, "It's kind of fun to do the impossible."

The success of the Disney Studio made Walt a multimillionaire. In 1949, the Disneys bought an estate in the Holmby Hills of Los Angeles. The home provided a magical kingdom to Diane and Sharon, whose father was not only fabulously wealthy but also the voice of the nation's beloved mouse.

Most people think of the father of the Disney empire as a benevolent figure, dedicated to making the mundane world a more enchanted one. However, life did not always imitate animation. His workers, unlike the seven dwarves, at one point refused to contentedly sing while toiling in the Disney gold mine. When they went on strike, Disney testified in front of the House Un-American Activities Committee and named several of his workers as communist sympathizers. Afterward, he instituted a blacklist at his studio. In Marc Eliot's biography, *Walt Disney: Hollywood's Dark Prince*, he writes that Disney served as a secret informer for the Los Angeles FBI until his death.

Just prior to Disney's passing, he established the California Institute of the Arts to help future artists. He said of his largesse, "It's the principal thing I hope to leave when I move on to greener pastures. If I can help provide a place to develop the talent of the future, I think I will have accomplished something."

The creator of the Magic Kingdom passed away from advanced lung cancer at age sixty-five, in 1966. If Walt Disney wanted to know what he had accomplished, he had merely to look upon his brainchild. Even when donning a sorcerer's hat, his four-fingered creation still retains animation's crown.

- The original family name was D'Isney, and they emigrated from Kilkenny, Ireland.
- Disney often called composer Robert B. Sherman into his office to play the piano for him. His favorite song was "Feed the Birds" from a Disney masterpiece, "Mary Poppins."
- Disney refused to allow Alfred Hitchcock to film at Disneyland because Hitchcock had made "that disgusting movie *Psycho.*"
- Disney served in his Red Cross unit with Ray Croc, the future founder of McDonald's.

- Disney holds the record of winning the most Academy Awards, with twenty-two wins in competitive categories.
- In 1983, Mickey donned a kimono for the dedication of Tokyo Disneyland; he sported a beret for the opening of Disneyland Paris.
- "Mickey Mouse" was the Allied forces' password on D-Day.

Eureka #16
(1927)

Prehistoric man left drawings on the caves in Lascaux, World War II servicemen penned "Kilroy was here," writer Johnston McCully had his hero Zorro leave his mark of "Z," and people everywhere feel the urge to write their names on any blank surface. It is our way of saying, "We were here. We mattered." One man, because of his eureka, was able to ward off oblivion and halt the relentless march of time.

Sidney Patrick was born in Indiana on March 17, 1879. Although the family was Jewish, his parents, because of the date of his birth, gave him an Irish middle name. Sid's father, David, was a minstrel, and as such, he followed the small-time show circuits. This livelihood resulted in a subsistence standard of living; therefore, with the advent of the California Gold Rush, David and the nineteen-year-old Sid headed for the Klondike. They failed to find gold in nugget form; however, they were successful in another venue. Sid soon perceived that the miners were stir crazy in Dawson City and were willing to part with gold for the lure of entertainment. Sid staged boxing matches in the famed Monte Carlo Saloon, which made him a handsome profit. After two years, they took their leave of the Yukon far wealthier than when they had arrived and made their way to San Francisco.

It was in this city that Sid saw his first movie at the Cinemagraph Theater. The motion picture industry was in its infancy, but Sid had learned the lesson of the Yukon: People will pay to be entertained. Accordingly, David and Sid purchased the Unique, a combination vaudeville and movie theater on Market Street. Its seating consisted of eight hundred kitchen chairs, and the only music came from a piano. It proved a profitable venture and boasted attractions such as Sophie Tucker, Al Jolson, and Roscoe "Fatty" Arbuckle, who started off as one of the theater's ticket takers. The Unique also had the distinction of premiering the West Coast debut of *The Great Train Robbery*. The Unique was destroyed by the San Francisco earthquake in 1906. However, Sid, after his initial shock, refused to be either bloodied or bowed. He managed to salvage one projector from the rubble and rented a huge tent from a traveling evangelist. He appropriated some pews from a ruined church for seating and, over the remains of the Unique, erected his tent with his hand-lettered sign: "Nothing to Fall on You but Canvass If There Is Another Quake." He sold ten thousand tickets a day.

When the show master realized that the true mecca of the burgeoning film industry was the City of Angels, he ditched his tent and headed to Los Angeles. There he entered into an arrangement with Hungarian Jewish immigrant and former furrier Adolph Zukor, the head of Paramount Pictures, to create a new theater. It was christened after Sid's surname and the amount of money lavished on his newest venture: Grauman's Million Dollar Theater. It was initially to be called the Rialto, but Sid ordered the name change: "When I spend that much money on a house, I want everybody to know it!" This was followed by the opening of his next theater in Hollywood, the Egyptian. In a brush with fortune, this coincided with the discovery of King Tut's tomb and so fed into the public's obsession with all things associated with the pharaoh. Sid gave the Egyptian a rectangular forecourt, a perfect place for stars to walk in the glow of klieg lights and for fans and photographers to ogle the celebrities as they paraded on the red carpet, a tradition that Sid instituted. However, all of his former temples were to pale before his greatest one.

Sid Grauman, fascinated with the east, decided the crown jewel of his career would be the apex of all theaters in terms of originality, architecture, cost, and showmanship. Thus from the glint in Sid's eyes was born Grauman's Chinese Theatre in Hollywood. Its ground-breaking ceremony took place on January 5, 1926, at 7:00 p.m. Silent screen star Norma Talmadge turned the first spadeful of earth with a gold-plated shovel. Celebrities in attendance were Fatty Arbuckle, Lon Chaney, Charles Chaplin, and Louis B. Mayer. Though the grand theater would become a movie-industry icon, Sid Grauman would soon have a rendezvous with serendipity that would be his true ticket to immortality.

In April 1927, Sid Grauman took Mary Pickford, Douglas Fairbanks, and Norma Talmadge to the construction site to check on the progress of the theater. As Norma alighted from the car, she stepped on the forecourt; however, as the cement had not yet dried, she left behind the imprint of her foot. Rather than being annoyed, Sid had his eureka moment: He would invite the reigning stars to likewise leave their footprints, thus immortalizing them in concrete. The master showman had come up with the greatest and longest-running publicity stunt in the history of the movies.

Sid made the inaugural footprint ceremony a public one, and on April 30, amid great fanfare, with the press in attendance, "America's Sweetheart" Mary Pickford made the first square. In the gray box she wrote, "Greetings to Sid," as well as her signature, and the year: "/27." It also contained her hand- and footprints. This was followed by her then husband, Douglas Fairbanks, who wrote, "Good luck Sid," along with his hand- and footprints. The second ceremony, on May 18, immortalized Norma Talmadge; although she was a silent film actress, her block on the forecourt would continue to speak for all time.

Today the forecourt of Grauman's Chinese Theatre is a mecca for pilgrims who love the movies and is the greatest collection of autographs in the world. A hallmark of celebrity status is an invitation to step into its wet cement. Jack Smith, a *Los Angeles Times* columnist, likened being asked to a ceremony at the forecourt as "the next best thing to sainthood."

The only person not associated with the entertainment industry to leave her mark was Rosa Grauman, Sid's mother, in 1940. Sid, who never married or had children, was extremely close with his mother, especially after the passing of his father in 1921. After his death, Rosa occupied a suite adjacent to her son's at the Ambassador Hotel, where Sid lived for many years. When she died, her bereft son continued on in his quarters and never parted with any of Rosa's clothes or personal effects. When asked why he placed his mother in the forecourt when she was not a celebrity, Sid replied, "Why not? She was a star to me." Sid received his own square in 1946. On it he wrote, "I am grateful to all who have made these hand and foot prints possible."

Hollywood, in turn, gave Sid Grauman his own red carpet treatment. At the twenty-first Academy Awards presentation, he was honored with a special Oscar for being a "master showman who raised the standard of exhibition of motion pictures." He was also made one of the thirty-six founding members of the academy. Hollywood's Last Emperor passed away from a heart attack in 1950. Grauman had wished that his mourners would send money to his favorite charities in lieu of flowers; however, his casket was surrounded by more than sixty floral pieces. One was in the shape of a heart, made of red roses. The name on the card was the one who had been responsible for Sid Grauman's eureka: Norma Talmadge.

The forecourt of Grauman's Chinese Theatre is Hollywood's sacred graffiti, a place where one can literally stand in the footprints of legends. The blocks are fossils; they say, "We were here. We mattered."

- In a classic *I Love Lucy* episode, Lucy and Ethel visit the forecourt and discover that the concrete block of John Wayne's square is loose. They attempt to steal it and take it home as a souvenir.
- Greta Garbo and Barbara Streisand, both averse to publicity, declined the invitation to leave their marks.

- Charlie Chaplin's square was removed from the forecourt in the early 1950s after he was branded a communist by Senator Joseph McCarthy. The theater managers explained that they had it removed because anticommunists covered it daily with garbage. The square had been made in 1928; Chaplin had left the imprints with his Little Tramp shoes. There was also the imprint of his cane. The whereabouts of the square is unknown.

- Sid Grauman, a practical joker, had once arranged for MGM's Marcus Loew to address an audience at the Ambassador Hotel. When Loew arrived, he discovered the room filled with wax figures borrowed from the nearby Hollywood Wax Museum.

- Marilyn Monroe said she used to go to the theater and try to fit her foot into the footprints of her favorite stars.

Eureka #17
(1937)

A honeymoon on a luxury liner can serve as a backdrop for romantic memories; however, in one instance, it served as the setting for a eureka moment. It was not the siren call of the sea but the rhythmic noise of the ship's engine that led to an epiphany, one that would delight future generations of the young as well as those young at heart.

Theodor Geisel grew up in Springfield, Massachusetts, a factory town that did not quite measure up to the poetry promised by its name. However, young Ted observed things that inspired him, such as the animals who lived in a local zoo, and he often drew them in his own whimsical fashion. His mother, Henrietta, encouraged his youthful endeavors. His childhood was a happy one, its only blight being animosity from neighbors. Because of World War I, Ted's parents, who were of German descent, were looked upon with suspicion. Moreover, his grandfather, who owned a brewery during Prohibition, was the target of anger from local residents.

After graduation, Ted attended Dartmouth College, where he was the editor of the campus humor magazine. This pastime was almost derailed when Ted had a drinking party in his room and the police were summoned. The school administrators forbade him to participate in any extracurricular activities. Ted got around this by publishing his articles under the pseudonym of Seuss, his mother's maiden name and his middle name.

After Dartmouth, Theodor entered Oxford University with the goal of becoming a professor, believing that was all he was going to be able to do with his Ivy League education. Sitting in class, Theodor was bored and spent his classes doodling whimsical animal drawings. These sketches were noticed by fellow American student Helen Palmer, who commented, "What you really want to do is draw." He took her advice and, soon after, her hand in marriage.

In the late 1920s, the couple moved to New York City, where Theodor sold his cartoons to *Vanity Fair* and the *Saturday Evening Post*. When one of his drawings was spotted by the wife of an advertising executive, she urged her husband to hire the talented illustrator, and subsequently, Ted spent the next thirteen years working at the ad company. One of his well-known slogans was for an insecticide: "Quick, Henry, the Flit!" His salary was substantial, and it enabled the Geisels to travel, which led to his eureka moment.

In 1937, Ted and Helen left New York Harbor on board a Swedish liner, the *Kungsholm*. On the return trip, a summer storm hammered the ship; Ted, rather than seek shelter in his cabin, strode the decks, hands gripping the rails. Later, while sipping vodka on the rocks, he became mesmerized by the repetitious rhythm of the ship's engines. This led to his eureka moment: He applied the incessant sound to a poem and afterward used the verse as the basis for a children's story.

The chanting of the engines led to the phrase, "And that is a story that no one can beat, and to think that I saw it on Mulberry Street." To accompany the words, he drew a young boy at a parade filled with fantastical creatures.

Perhaps one of the reasons Geisel was so enthralled by the engines' sound was that they were similar to one of his childhood memories: His adored mother had worked in her father's bakery, and to help her remember the names of the pies, she would chant them to her customers. Later, she would apply the same technique with bedtime stories when her young son had trouble falling asleep. Ted credited his mother "for the rhythms in which I write and the urgency with which I do it."

Ted, with Helen's steadfast encouragement, decided to try to get his shipboard story published. Twenty-nine publishers rejected his book. Their standard comment was "the book is too different" or "fantasy is not saleable." Ted argued that it wasn't fantasy because Mulberry Street was located in Springfield, and the parade had been derived from his recollections of his childhood hometown. Dejected, he planned a ceremonial burning of the tattered manuscript at his apartment. As chance would have it, he walked along Madison Avenue and ran into an old classmate from Dartmouth, Mike McClintock, who only hours before had been made juvenile editor of Vanguard Press. He invited Ted to come to his office, and half an hour later, he agreed to publish the book. If Ted had been walking in the other direction on Madison, he probably would have ended up forever creating variations of "Quick, Henry, the Flit!"

Geisel decided to publish the book under his old Dartmouth pseudonym of Seuss; he added "Dr." in a tongue-in-cheek nod to his abandoned Oxford doctorate. Ted named the boy in the story Marcos, after McClintock's son; it was also dedicated to Marcos.

When the book came out, Beatrix Potter, the creator of Peter Rabbit, praised it as near-perfect art. Dr. Seuss had taken his first step on the rhyming road of literary legend. However, his greatest work was yet to come.

In 1954, *Life* magazine published an article called "Why Johnny Can't Read"; it blamed the problem on the boring early primers. It called them "antiseptic" and the children in them "unnaturally clean." At that time, the standard childhood primers featured Dick, Jane, and their dog, Spot. Not only was there nothing fantastical about them, but the characters consisted of a middle-class, white nuclear family. This situation prompted McClintock to send Geisel a list of 250 words that children should know, and told him to write a story using only them. Nine months later was born literature's famous feline: *The Cat in the Hat.*

A subsequent chapter in Dr. Seuss' life proved that even exorbitant wealth, fame, and acclaim cannot serve as armor against grief. Since 1954, his wife, Helen, had been suffering from Guillain-Barré syndrome and experiencing excruciating pain in her legs and feet. This was followed by a number of other illnesses, including cancer.

During this time, the couple was living in a renovated observation tower in La Jolla, California, and Ted was having an affair with Audrey Dimond, the wife of a cardiologist. The two couples had long been friends. Indeed, Ted had dedicated *Fox in Socks* (1965) to Mitzi Long and Audrey Dimond of the Mt. Soledad Lingual Laboratories. In 1967, Helen committed suicide by taking an overdose of pills. She suspected the affair, and her last desperate act may have been to release her husband so he would no longer be saddled with a terminally ill spouse.

Eight months after Helen died, Ted moved into a hotel in Reno with Audrey. He said, "My best friend is being divorced, and I'm going to Reno to comfort his wife." It was pure Seussian logic, but as with his fiction, it worked pure magic.

Audrey brought her two daughters into the marriage but had none with Ted. When asked why the famous writer of children's books had no offspring of his own, his stock response was, "You make 'em and I'll entertain 'em." Audrey Geisel said that the suicide and rapid remarriage caused "a rather large ripple in the community of La Jolla." However, Ted's philosophy of the scandal can best be described by one of his quotations: "Be who you are and say what you feel, because those who mind don't matter, and those who matter don't mind." His 1984 book, *Butter Battle Book*, bore the dedication "For Audrey, With Love."

Just as the sea outside the tower beat ceaselessly on, so did time. As Seuss had once written, "How did it get so late so soon?" At age eighty-seven, the author passed away from cancer. However, the doctor's prescription for a world of fancy and fun lives on: a kingdom where green eggs are served, felines wear hats, and a grinch has a heart three sizes too small. For making our lives a more wonderful place, we should tip our hats, striped or otherwise, to Dr. Seuss.

- In his adopted hometown of San Diego, the University of California has a Geisel Library. It contains the original sketches for *The Cat in the Hat* and has a bronze statue showing Ted sitting at his desk in the tower, with one of his legs on its top and the Cat in the Hat standing behind him. His wife Audrey said of it, "It's perfect because that man never had both feet on the ground. One leg represents reality, the other is his imagination."
- Forty-four Dr. Seuss books have been translated into twenty-one languages and have sold more than 500 million copies. His website—maintained by his publisher, Random House—receives 100,000 hits a day.
- Geisel won an Academy Award in 1947 for a documentary feature, made when he was in the Animation Department of the army's First Motion Picture Unit.
- The Geisel estate continues to receive $13 million a year from royalties from Dr. Seuss books and merchandising.

Eureka #18
(1934)

Revolutions have made deep inroads on the face of history: The French, American, and Russian revolutions irrevocably altered the world. However, there was another type of upheaval, equally ideological but far less bloody, that led not to political change but to intellectual revolution. Moreover, in the process, a bird once only indigenous to the Arctic became ubiquitous throughout the world.

At Bristol Grammar School, Allen Williams was an indifferent student who would never have had a life intimately involved with books except for an event that altered his destiny. When Allen was a teenager, his uncle, John Lane, told the Williams family that because he was childless, he would look upon Allen as his surrogate son if he agreed to change his surname to Lane. Not only did Allen agree to this but the whole family changed their name as well. Excited to leave school, where he had achieved only mediocrity, Allen Lane left home at age sixteen to seek his fortune in London.

Allen began his publishing apprenticeship at the Bodley

Head publishing house, where John Lane held the reins firmly in his hands; eschewing nepotism, he started his nephew off at the bottom rung. Bodley Head had among its roster of high-profile clients Oscar Wilde; however, no love was lost, or ever found for that matter, between John Lane and Wilde. Lane was furious with the writer because he had seduced an office boy from Bodley Head; Wilde showed his reciprocal contempt by calling a manservant Lane in *The Importance of Being Earnest.*

Because of Allen's connections, he was given the privilege of meeting authors such as Bernard Shaw and Anatole France. As a member of a horse-riding club, he was also invited to attend a gala at Buckingham Palace, in full equestrian attire. His spurs locked together and, when summoned to meet the king, he glided forward in a gait more suited to a slow-motion ice-skater.

In 1923, John Lane died, and his will stipulated that the Bodley Head torch be left to his young heir apparent. The first major butting of heads in the company occurred over the banning of *Ulysses*; the threat of prosecution made it a literary hot potato. When Allen decided that Bodley Head was going to publish it, his board of directors was equally committed that it would not. Its publication proved both a commercial and literary victory.

In 1934, after a weekend in Devon visiting Agatha Christie, Allen found himself bookless, waiting for a train. Desperate for reading material, he discovered that he could not find anything to read at the station bookstall except pulp paperbacks and popular magazines. It was then that Allen had his eureka moment: He realized his mission, for both missionary and mercenary reasons, would be to satiate the public's appetite for inexpensive, quality books. At that time, the only source for reading contemporary authors was through hardback editions, which were so expensive they were out of reach for the common man. Allen immediately grasped that there was a huge need for affordable, quality literature, which would mean distributing the works as paperbacks. He felt that they should be priced the same as a pack of cigarettes and small enough to slip into a pocket. He later explained, "A man who may be poor in money is not necessarily poor in intellectual qualities."

His colleagues not only did not share his enthusiasm but were dead set against it; they felt that literature was the realm of the moneyed, not the masses. Allen, realizing he could march to no other drummer than his own, decided to forfeit his inheritance and leave his uncle's press.

With his brothers and £100, Allen set out to found his own publishing enterprise; he rented space in the crypt of Holy Trinity Church and arranged for a fairground slide to receive deliveries from the street above. Once settled in, he needed to christen his company. When his secretary suggested the name Penguin, Allen Lane latched onto it; he felt that it was "dignified but flippant." The twenty-two-year-old Edward Young, who had been lured away from Bodley Head to design dust jackets, was immediately dispatched to the zoo in Regents Park for inspiration for a logo.

Lane decided that he wanted his books to be taken seriously; consequently, they would not have any pictures on their covers because that would have been too similar to the lurid paperbacks then sold. Once he had the place, the name, and the design, all Allen needed was customers.

Customers, however, proved to be a sticking point in Allen's plan, as many booksellers refused to stock the paperbacks. Allen felt he was going to have to admit defeat when serendipity stepped in.

The buyer for the chain store Woolworth's told Allen that he did not like books without pictures on their covers, but at that moment, the buyer's wife showed interest in the product, so he agreed to carry a few dozen copies for each of the London stores. Due to their success, Woolworth's placed another order a few weeks later, this time for over 63,000 copies. The seemingly flightless bird was flying off the shelves.

The "dignified but flippant" publisher became as much a British national institution as the BBC, the Old Vic, and the Rolls-Royce. Lane had become the modern Gutenberg. Early editorial meetings were held in a favorite Spanish restaurant, the Barcelona, with plenty of wine to accompany them. One visitor was shocked to discover an editorial meeting taking place on a rowboat, the staff dipping into gin as steadily as the oars did into the water. Allen Lane became a millionaire and the prophet of a publishing revolution.

In 1941, Allen was in Cambridge for an editorial meeting when he attended a party. He was standing by himself, as his social skills did not match his entrepreneurial ones. One of the guests, Lettice Orr, noticed the impressive, meticulously tweed-clad publisher, and a week later Allen invited her to stay at Silverbeck, the mansion that Penguin had built. The estate was flanked by a huge wrought-iron gate, either side decorated with his trademark birds. They were married later that year, a contingent of cardboard Penguins forming a guard of honor outside the church. They had three daughters, and Allen proved every inch the doting father. Further fame followed when he was knighted; on this Buckingham Palace visit he forwent spurs.

In 1960, Lane once again became the champion of free speech when he decided that Penguin would publish the unexpurgated version of D. H. Lawrence's steamy *Lady Chatterley's Lover.* The trial for obscenity was decided by Mervyn Griffith-Jones, who, when asked how he would decide whether or not to prosecute, answered, "I'll put my feet up on the desk and start reading. If I get an erection, we prosecute." Lane was ultimately acquitted, and sales soared to 3 million. The second edition of the novel contained a dedication from Penguin publishers to the intrepid jurors.

Although fortune smiled on Lane on the professional front, his home life did not fare as well; by the mid-1950s, his marriage was unraveling. This was partially due to Lane's coldness. As he himself remarked, even those he loved "could only get so close, but no closer."

In 1965, chief editor Tony Godwin bought a book titled, perhaps symbolically, *Massacre*, which Lane thought unworthy of Penguin's imprint. Allen, along with some long-serving, loyal members of the warehouse staff, loaded all the offending books from the Penguin storeroom into a van and burned them. He then sacked Godwin and retained control of his company.

In 1970, Sir Allen Lane finally met an opponent he could not knock down; he passed away from bowel cancer, and his ashes were interred, alongside his uncle John's and his parents', in the graveyard of an ancient monastery on the North Devon coast. Tributes flooded in from all over the literary world; obituaries were long and laudatory. The most heartfelt tribute came from Allen's son-in-law, Clare's husband, Michael Morpurgo: "AL's epitaph might be the same as Christopher Wren's, 'If you seek his monument, look around you.' He was kind and ruthless, charming and chilling, generous and mean, a complex man, never easy to understand. But heroes should be judged, I think, by what they achieve. It should be added, as a footnote but an important one, that Allen Lane is also my wife's great hero. Being her father, I suppose, that's hardly surprising."

Sir Allen Lane, the literary emperor penguin, hatched his brainchild in a British train station. In turn, it gave birth to a twentieth-century revolution waged with ink rather than blood, and resulted in the democratization of knowledge.

- In 1937, Penguin moved its office from its crypt to Middlesex; the property cost £2,000, plus an additional £200 for the crop of cabbages that were growing there. The staff had to pick its way through the cabbages, which Lane marketed. The location is opposite to what is now Heathrow Airport. Allen's father laid the cornerstone of the new building.
- An annual Penguin festival takes place in Bristol (May 18–21), the city of Allen's birth.
- Allen's brother John was killed in the North Africa Landings in 1942. In 1955, his brother Richard took over Penguin in Australia. (He made a huge mistake when he sold his personal shares.)
- Penguin continues Allen Lane's tradition of championing free speech with titles such as Salman Rushdie's *Satanic Verses*. The company also released Michael Moore's *Stupid White Men* after attempts in the United States to ban it.

Eureka #19
(1935)

Lists of twentieth-century heroes always include Mother Teresa, Mohandas Gandhi, Nelson Mandela, and Dr. Martin Luther King Jr. However, there is another hero whose name is mainly unfamiliar to those outside his circle of disciples. This is because he embraced anonymity as one of his tenets, in order to deflect personal glory to the greater good of his cause—a cause that was born from his soul-saving eureka moment.

The man who was to state that he was "just another drunk" was born in 1895 in a small room behind a bar in a Vermont mining town. The rocky landscape of his youth was to prove a metaphor for Bill Wilson's life.

The Wilson family's descent into misery occurred when William was ten years old and his father, an alcoholic philanderer, embarked on a permanent business trip. His mother, not relishing her role as deserted wife, left her children with her parents. Another tragedy was when his first love died after a minor surgery, when he was seventeen. The loss of his parents, girlfriend, and home sent Bill spiraling into a sea of depression. What helped rescue him from the depths was when he married Lois Burnham. His bride was the daughter of a surgeon, and she was raised in an affluent neighborhood in Brooklyn Heights. She later described her childhood as "idyllic."

In 1917, Bill was conscripted into the army, and though he never saw combat, he came back mortally wounded. In England, the first butler he had ever seen gave him his first drink, a Bronx Cocktail, and he was instantly smitten. While some people find messages in a bottle, Bill believed he had found escape in one. He later stated of his love affair with alcohol, "I had found the elixir of life." When Bill returned, although outwardly unchanged, inside he was a different man. He was addicted to St. Booze. Bill's dependency was so great that he did not graduate from law school because he was too drunk to pick up his diploma. Instead, he became a stock speculator, and he and Lois traveled the country on a motorcycle odyssey.

Friends felt "a lunacy commission should be appointed"; however, the business proved prosperous. Lois hoped that getting Bill out of his habitual environment would curb his drinking, but this did not prove to be the case. To allay his wife's misgivings, he assured her that men of genius conceived their best ideas while intoxicated. When his friends started to lecture him, he withdrew from them. Similarly, because of his drinking, there were extremely unpleasant scenes in the Wilson home. Years later, at the tail end of Bill's downward spiral into an alcoholic abyss, when he collapsed in a stupor in the hallway of their Brooklyn house, Lois had reached the proverbial last straw. She pounded hysterically on his chest and screamed, "You don't even have the decency to die!" Nevertheless, despite this episode, she devoted her life to her husband's salvation.

With the fall of the stock market, Bill and Lois had to move in with her parents. When Lois was asleep, Bill would steal money from her purse and hit the bars. She continued to believe if she just loved him enough, he would be cured. To compound matters, their house was foreclosed, Lois' mother died, her father became ill, and she suffered a number of devastating miscarriages.

To try to stop his descent, Bill's brother-in-law arranged for him to enter a renowned hospital for the treatment of alcoholism. Upon release, he fell off the wagon and was readmitted. Lois was informed by the staff that her husband would soon end up in an asylum or with an undertaker.

In November 1934, Bill was drinking when he received a phone call from an old school friend and drinking buddy, Ebby Thatcher. He invited him over, eager to have someone to get drunk with. However, when Ebby arrived, he was sober, and boasted he had been so for weeks. He claimed he did it because he had found religion. Bill thought to himself, "Last summer an alcoholic crackpot; now, I suspected, a little cracked about religion." Ebby explained he had found salvation in the evangelical Christian Oxford Group and had come to New York to get Bill involved. This failed as well, and Bill was readmitted to the hospital again.

There Bill had an out-of-body experience. An avowed agnostic, Wilson refused to give it a religious slant; instead, he referred to it as his hot flash. He stated that while lying in bed, mired in depression, he cried out, "I'll do anything! Anything at all! If there be a God, let Him show Himself!" He then felt the sensation of a bright light, followed by a long-forgotten sense of serenity. Bill Wilson never drank again.

Bill's epiphany gave him fresh resolve, and he had been sober for five months when he found himself on a business trip in Akron, Ohio, where, in homing-pigeon fashion, he felt himself drawn to the Mayflower Hotel's bar. Before he entered, Bill had his eureka moment: Only a drunk can help another drunk. He realized that he might be able to maintain his own sobriety if he could help another drunk deny his drink.

Through the intervention of an Oxford Group member named Henrietta Seiberling, Wilson contacted Dr. Robert Holbrook Smith on Mother's Day 1935. The Dartmouth-educated physician, because of his alcoholism, did not have much left of his medical practice, his finances, or his reputation. Skeptical of meeting a stranger based on their common affliction, Bob Smith met with Bill Wilson, explaining that he could only stay for fifteen minutes. He stayed six hours. Through one another's empathy, the two men were able to overcome the demon of alcoholism. The following month, on June 10, the date Alcoholics Anonymous recognizes as its official founding, Bob Smith had his last drink. It was a beer followed by a tranquilizer. He needed them to steady his hands—he was about to perform an operation.

Smith and Wilson realized that they had stumbled on the way to help fellow sufferers. The meeting between the two men was one of the most spiritually significant of the century.

Wilson began each AA meeting with the phrase, "My name is Bill W., and I'm an alcoholic." He started the tradition to provide his members anonymity, something he wanted for himself as well. In keeping with his organization's adherence to confidentiality, Wilson turned down an honorary degree from Yale University and refused to allow his photograph, even from the back, to be on the cover of *Time* magazine.

However, his control of his alcoholism did not prove to be a cure-all for the ills in his life. Bill was a serial adulterer. After meetings where he preached his twelve steps, his thirteenth step was a sexual liaison with recovering younger women. His staff, aware of his philandering and fearing its detrimental effects on their organization, organized a Founder's Watch, where they kept an eye on Wilson during the fraternizing that followed AA functions.

In the mid-1950s, one of these affairs, with a woman named Helen Wynn, stepped into the arena of emotional adultery; it lasted fifteen years. He admitted that "in duration, intensity and scope," she was different from all his other women. The forty-year-old divorcée, a former actress, was as smitten with her lover as he was with her. However, after putting his wife, Lois, through twelve layers (or steps) of hell, he could not find it in his heart to abandon her.

Helen eventually bought a house in Ireland. Although she was gone, she was not forgotten. In his will, Bill left 10 percent of all book royalties from *Alcoholics Anonymous* to Helen Wynn. The other 90 percent was bequeathed to Lois Wilson. As millions of the books sold, the bequest turned into a substantial amount of money.

After setting up a hierarchy of leadership for Alcoholics Anonymous, in 1955, Wilson handed over the leadership of his organization at the St. Louis National Convention. He told his foundation that "Alcoholics Anonymous was safe—even from me." His parting words: "Let go and let God."

Bill and Lois bought a house they christened Stepping Stones on an eight-acre estate in Bedford Hill, New York. The house is open for tours and is on the National Register of Historic Places. There the addictive personality began his final addiction, this time to nicotine. He became a chain-smoker; and as he had once done with the bottle, he squirreled away his cigarettes from Lois. He contracted emphysema and later pneumonia. Undeterred, he alternated inhaling cigarette smoke and inhaling from his oxygen tank.

On his deathbed, Bill Wilson did not experience another quasi-religious experience. Nor did he call out for his wife or his long lost love, Helen. Rather, although he had not had a drink in thirty-five years, he called out for whiskey. His last request was not granted.

Bill Wilson's eureka moment in a hotel lobby became a life preserver for millions. In light of this, his comment that he was "just another drunk" was hardly an astute self-analysis. His brainchild, Alcoholics Anonymous, has enabled addicts the world over to "let go and let god."

- *Alcoholics Anonymous* had a number of provisional titles, among them *The Way Out* and *The Empty Glass*.
- Lois Wilson was the founder of Al-Anon, a support group for the loved ones of those addicted to alcohol.
- Author Aldous Huxley proclaimed that Bill Wilson was "the greatest social architect of the century."
- In the 1950s, Wilson and Aldous Huxley began to experiment with LSD; Bill was so enthused he wanted to distribute it at AA meetings. His staff was able to dissuade him.

- Wilson became involved with spiritualism. He stated that when writing *Twelve Steps and Twelve Traditions*, he arrived at the number twelve after the twelve apostles. He also had a spook room in his basement, where he conducted séances with a Ouija board.

Eureka #20
(1938)

Sometimes inspiration whispers into a creator's ears with the majesty equivalent to the panel on the Sistine Chapel wherein God breathes life into Adam. On the other hand, sometimes the muse, in true flirtatious fashion, camouflages herself as a homely girl until she reveals her true beauty underneath. This latter situation was the case when an ordinary event led to an icon.

In 1938, a New York City high school English teacher, Murray Burnett, traveled to Europe, accompanied by his wife, Frances. The trip was undertaken so that Murray, who was Jewish, could help his relatives smuggle valuables from Nazi-occupied Vienna. Murray came away having witnessed the plight of the thousands of refugees desperately trying to flee the Nazis.

Before the Burnetts returned home, they made a stopover at Cap Ferrat, a resort town in the south of France, where they visited a nightclub, La Belle Aurore. There a black pianist played jazz for an eclectic audience, which consisted of

French guests, refugees from various countries, and the new lords of the land, the Nazis. The scene prompted Murray's eureka moment: As he sat there, amid the assorted cast of characters, the exotic locale, and the specter of the Third Reich, Burnett told his wife, "What a setting for a play!"

Once back in the States, he and his friend Joan Alison, a socialite heiress and occasional playwright, decided to commit his experience to paper, with the main setting that had ignited his inspiration, La Belle Aurore. As he explained, "The nightclub was a great contrast to the tragedy and the tears. It was a gay, happy atmosphere.... Here was Hitler and there was no question they were on the brink of terror, not only anti-Semitic terror, but terror and war, and no one gave a damn."

Murray had the piano player in the French bar sing his own favorite song—"As Time Goes By"—one that he listened to so often during his senior year at Cornell University that he had worn out his recording. Murray resurrected the music and employed it as the bittersweet love song between the play's two central characters.

Murray based the principal character, Rick, on his ideal rather than his real personality. Murray viewed himself as the rather passive son who had always been under the control of his overprotective mother and who had taken the safe track of Ivy League school and a respectable job working in the same city where he was raised. In contrast, Rick was the owner of an exotic bar, where he controlled the destinies of its clientele and, though professing to "stick his neck out for no one," ultimately sacrificed his chance with the love of his life for the cause of a greater good.

Murray and Joan completed their six-act play in as many weeks; their agent, Anne Watkins, sold it in one. It was picked up by theater producers Martin Gabel and Carly Wharton. However, a problem arose when Wharton wanted Murray to change the part where Ilsa, a young wife desperate for transit papers for herself and her husband, offers herself to the nightclub owner, Rick, in exchange for escape from Casablanca.

When Murray and Joan refused the rewrite, the option was dropped. Their agent then suggested that they should try to sell it to Hollywood. The typed script then sat for a year until it was discovered by Irene Lee, who headed the story department for Warner Bros. Three weeks later, the studio bought the play *Everyone Comes to Rick's* for $20,000, which was the highest sum the studio had ever paid for an unpublished play. They gave the task of converting the material into a screenplay to twin brothers, Julian and Philip Epstein, and Howard Koch, who changed its name to *Casablanca*.

Burnett's golden dialogue lit up the silver screen, as did the mesmerizing performances of Humphrey Bogart and Ingrid Bergman. Further contributing to its success was its topicality: Its release in November 1942 coincided with the Allied landing and summit conference in the North African city. Moreover, its strongly anti-Nazi story with the star-crossed lovers separated by the war made it the most popular film of its time.

It was at this juncture that the seamy underbelly of *Casablanca* reared its head. The movie made superstar status of Bogart and Bergman, as well as the Epstein twins, and Howard Koch won an Academy Award for Best Screenplay. Ironically, nowhere in the acclaim for the movie, which became the main jewel in the Warner Bros. crown, was any recognition given to the screenplay's true creator, Murray Burnett. The writer felt like Esau, cheated out of his birthright. However, what he was deprived of was far greater than a "mess of potage"; it was recognition for being the creator of one of the most iconic classics in movie history.

When Koch was quoted in an article for *New York* magazine that the original play merely provided his script's exotic locale and a character named Rick, Burnett and Alison were incensed. Murray said of Koch after reading it, "Koch took credit for everything. He says he took this magic pencil, Eagle Number One, and he wrote it line by line. But every character in the film is in my play. Every one. Without exception."

Burnett sued Koch and the magazine for $6.5 million apiece. He was unsuccessful in receiving any compensation. The court's decision was based on its belief that Koch's statements had not libeled Burnett or his play. He then sued Warner Bros. to get back the right to his characters. He lost. Undeterred, he spent the next eighteen years on his crusade to reclaim his lost literary child.

In 1990, he was still on his mission. He spoke against the myth that his play had provided no more than a character named Rick. However, a year later, almost half a century after what he always claimed was the theft of his brainchild, a then eighty-nine-year-old Howard Koch capitulated to the truth. He stated in a letter in the *Los Angeles Times*, "Having read the play more recently, I believe that the complaint was, to some extent, justified. After fifty years, memories can be faulty." He went on to elaborate that he had merely been handed a script by the Epstein brothers and had just assumed they were the playwrights. Murray Burnett at last had his vindication, and monetary compensation was soon to follow.

When Burnett and Alison threatened not to renew their original agreement with Warner Bros. when it was slated to expire in 1997, they received $100,000. The retired schoolteacher felt that justice delayed was justice nevertheless. Although embroiled in a custody battle over *Casablanca*, Murray still had nothing but the highest admiration for the film. He called it "true yesterday, true today, true tomorrow." Murray Burnett died soon after, at age eighty-six, comforted in the knowledge that he had created *Casablanca*.

The saying "success has many fathers" was very much the case with *Casablanca*. It took a great number of fortuitous events for the silver screen masterpiece to be born. However, its conception came from a eureka moment by a schoolteacher experiencing firsthand the horrors of Nazism. Little did Murray Burnett know when he left for Europe that he would soon be giving the world one of its most enduring love stories, one that would continue even "as time goes by."

- Murray Burnett's second wife was Adrienne Bayah. Upon her husband's death, she donated the original copy of his play, *Everyone Comes to Rick's*, to a film institute.
- The first studio to be interested in *Everyone Comes to Rick's* was MGM, but studio boss Louis B. Mayer refused to pay the $5,000 fee.
- *Casablanca* won three Academy Awards in 1943, including Best Picture.

Eureka #21
(1939)

Fairy tales innocuously begin with "Once upon a time" and contain some of the most terrifying antagonists in literature: the Queen in *Snow White*, the witch in *Hansel and Gretel*, the Big Bad Wolf in *Little Red Riding Hood*. However, in one modern-day classic tale, no malevolent characters darken its pages. Perhaps this was because the authors' actual world was so rife with horror, they were loath to let any of it seep into their books.

Hans Augusto Reyersbach was born in Germany in close proximity to the Hagenbeck Zoo. There he developed a life-long love of animals and would spend many afternoons sketching them. His innocent childhood later proved to be a sharp contrast to his teen years; he was drafted into service in World War I, where he served in the infantry in France and Russia. With his country's defeat, he returned to Germany, which had been brought to its knees.

Hans attended the universities of Munich and Hamburg, and afterward worked as a lithographer, specializing in posters for circuses, once again drawing his beloved animals. In the early 1920s, he attended a party at his girlfriend's home, where he saw her younger sister, Margarete Elisabeth Waldstein, sliding down a banister. Little did the two know that their destinies were to become intertwined.

Due to the crippling inflation in Germany in 1924, Hans decided to carve out his economic niche elsewhere. He packed up his sketchbooks, his paintbrushes, and his pipe, and he headed for Brazil. The six-foot-two, pale-skinned foreigner, with his big hat to protect his balding head from the scorching Brazilian sun, cut a unique figure in his adopted country. Hans made his living selling sinks and bathtubs up and down the Amazon River. On his travels, he again observed monkeys, this time sans bars. And, as he had done as a child, he drew endless sketches of them.

In 1935, he was reunited with the banister-sliding girl, who had left Hamburg to escape its anti-Semitism. They were drawn together because of their shared commonalities: religion, country of origin, love of animals, and art. Margarete convinced Hans to abandon his business, and together they formed the first advertising agency in Rio. Hans also found work for the advertising firm of Hoffman-La Roche, and drew maps and posters, illustrated cookbooks, and designed Christmas cards for corporate clients. The couple married and shared their apartment with two pet marmosets, which were always getting into mischief. Because the Brazilians had difficulty pronouncing their names, Margarete shortened her name to Margret and Hans Reyersbach shortened his surname to Rey.

After their two-week honeymoon in Paris, they were so

smitten with the city they relocated there and lived in a hotel in Montmartre. Hans and Margret would take walks along the banks of the Seine; stop at local cafés; and, of course, visit the zoo. As their two beloved pet monkeys had died on the passage to Europe, the couple adopted two French turtles: Claude and Claudius.

To earn money, Hans drew cartoon characters for a newspaper, one of which was so engaging that in 1939 he was contacted by a French publisher to expand his drawings into a book. The result was *Raffy and the Nine Monkeys*. Its pages debuted the animal that had captured his imagination when he first saw it at the Hagenbeck Zoo, a mischievous monkey he named Fifi. As the impish character became popular with French children, Hans and Margret, who always thought as one, had a shared eureka moment: They realized they had a creation who could become a beloved children's character. Thus, Hans decided to write another book, this time based on the monkey and his adventures or, more precisely, his misadventures.

Their shared eureka evolved into *The Adventures of Fifi*. For its title page, Hans drew a picture of Fifi sitting in a tree at a zoo. In his hand was the string of a red balloon. He signed the page in small black letters: H. A. Rey—Paris Jan. 1940. Their plans for the book, however, were interrupted; soldiers were on the verge of invading France. As both Hans and Margret were German Jews, they knew that if captured they would be sent to a concentration camp. Again Hans packed his sketchbooks, his paintbrushes, and his pipe. However, this time he included something else: his manuscript of *The Adventures of Fifi*. The childhood innocence of the irrepressible monkey was in sharp contrast to the unimaginable evil that shadowed Hans and Margret's escape from Europe.

As the Reys did not own a car, and the trains were no longer running, they went to a bicycle shop for their means of escape. All that was left was a tandem bicycle, which Margret was unable to maneuver. The owner, taking advantage of their plight, sold them spare parts that were lying around the shop for 1,600 francs, almost a month's lodging. Hans built makeshift bikes, and in June 1940, the Reys joined the throng of 5 million fleeing refugees, all desperate to leave before the arrival of the Nazis. Although the Reys were soon exhausted from the heat and the chaos, they were propelled forward by the drone of the German planes circling overhead. Some of their nights were spent on a bed of hay in a stable with cows, on the floor of a school, and in a French restaurant. With relief, the Reys finally boarded a train in Orléans that would carry them to Spain and then Portugal. They sailed back to Brazil aboard the *Angola.*

Once back in Rio de Janeiro, the Reys decided to move to the United States. Perhaps they wanted to be closer to family—Margret had a sister who lived near New York City. Or perhaps, after having endured political trouble in Germany and Paris, they thought America would be more stable. Once again, Hans packed up his essentials.

On October 14, four months after their harrowing bicycle escape from Paris, the Reys, along with Fifi, saw the Statue of Liberty. Although they had very little money and no jobs, they had each other and their talent. They felt that was enough for a great beginning. One year later, their book was picked up by a new editor at Houghton Mifflin, Grace Hogarth, whom the

Reys had known when she was a children's book editor at their British publisher, Chatto and Windus. She had also fled Europe because of World War II.

The book would bring Hans, Margret, and their brainchild enduring fame and wealth, not only in their new country but throughout the world. Like Hans Augusto Reyersbach and Margarete Waldstein, Fifi would also undergo a name change: Curious George. The adjective "curious" was a description for his inquisitive nature and his most curious origin.

"Call me Ishmael" are the three famous words that begin *Moby-Dick*; "This is George" are the three famous words that begin *Curious George*. While the former is a perennial favorite among adults, the latter is beloved among children. In trying to explain George's enduring appeal, Margret stated, "George can do what kids can't do. He can hang from a kite in the sky. He can let the animals out of their pens on the farm. He can do all these naughty things that kids would like to do." She concluded by saying that they received their inspiration by looking at the child who still lived within both husband and wife. "I'm proud of you, George," the man with the yellow hat says in *Curious George Gets a Medal*. "I guess the whole world is proud of you today." For creating their literary icon against a backdrop of horror, it is a medal George's creators are equally deserving of.

In 1977, Hans passed away, leaving his beloved Margret and George. His widow was left to shoulder on without the man in the big hat whom she had loved for almost half a century. Although both Hans and Margret are no longer alive, they live on in their irrepressible fictional child: Curious George, born from their shared eureka moment.

- Margret and Hans loved animals and owned, at various times, turtles, monkeys, alligators, chameleons, newts, and dogs (always cocker spaniels).
- *Curious George* has been published with different names. He started off in France as Fifi. A British publisher, in deference to the reigning English king, changed his name from George to Zozo; "curious" was also omitted from his name, as this was a slang word for "gay" in London.
- After she became a widow, Margret continued to write and became a professor of creative writing at Brandeis University.
- In 1980, Margret began collaborating with Alan Shalleck on a series of short films featuring Curious George. One hundred short episodes aired on the Disney Channel. Shalleck was later murdered as a result of a home robbery.
- The first seven books all had the same opening line, "This is George."

Eureka #22
(1941)

Throughout the pages of history, there have always been memorable fictional females: Margaret Mitchell's Scarlett O'Hara, Leo Tolstoy's Anna Karenina, Gustave Flaubert's Emma Bovary, and Jane Austen's Elizabeth Bennet. However, there is one heroine, born from a wife's eureka and her husband's imagination, who, although possessing the appearance of a sexpot, could, on any level, take on even the most alpha of males.

William Moulton Marston was a Renaissance man: He earned a law degree and a doctorate in psychology, and published *Emotions of Normal People*. He also made a significant scientific contribution when his wife, Elizabeth, remarked to him that when she "became angry or excited her blood pressure seemed to climb." This sparked an idea in her husband, resulting in his developing the polygraph (otherwise known as the lie detector). However, his brow was to be crowned with another laurel, again with an impetus from Elizabeth.

In 1940, Olive Byrne (his former student from Tufts) interviewed Dr. Marston for the magazine *Family Circle.* The piece was titled "Don't Laugh at the Comics," and in it he promoted the concept that comics possessed educational potential as they at least got kids reading. This was in contrast to child psychiatrist Frederic Wertham, who felt Superman would never compare with Shakespeare. The article caught the attention of Maxwell Charles Gaines, who hired Marston as a consultant for his company, DC Comics.

At that time, the comic industry was dominated by superheroes such as Green Lantern, Batman, and Superman. Marston decided to create his own character; however, he envisioned the character as one who would triumph not with *Bam!* and *Ka-Runch!* but with the force of love. Once again his wife, Elizabeth, was the catalyst for his creation. Her eureka moment was when she responded to his idea to make a less violent superhero: "Fine. But make her a woman."

William wanted to create a superheroine who would serve as a role model for girls. Finding his character took some thought; she did not spring full-blown from his head as Athena had from Zeus.

However, for his inspiration he needed to look no farther than his wife, Elizabeth (Sadie) Holloway Marston. In an era when most women did not attend university, Elizabeth obtained a master's degree in psychology from Holyoke College. When William entered Harvard to study law, she wanted to join him, but the Ivy League university excluded women. Instead, women had to go to Harvard's sister school, Radcliffe. Elizabeth rejected that choice, dismissing it as "lovely law for ladies," and headed instead to Boston University.

Her father refused to lend her $100 for tuition with the

words, "Absolutely not. As long as I have money to keep you in aprons, you can stay home with your mother." Mr. Holloway was a creature of his time; his daughter was not. Undeterred, Elizabeth sold cookbooks to the local ladies' club until she had the required funds. Elizabeth earned her law degree in 1918, one of three women to graduate. As she later recounted, "I finished the Massachusetts Bar exam in nothing flat and had to go out and sit on the stairs waiting for Bill and another Harvard man . . . to finish."

Postgraduation, Elizabeth embarked on a thirty-five-year working career. Some of her jobs included indexing the documents of the first fourteen Congresses; lecturing on law, ethics, and psychology at New York universities; and working as an editor for *Encyclopedia Britannica* and *McCall's* magazine. She also cowrote a textbook, *Integrative Psychology.* She waited until age thirty-five to have her first baby and then promptly returned to work.

In 1933, Elizabeth landed a position as assistant to the chief executive of Metropolitan Life Insurance Company in New York, which supported her family during the Depression when her husband was without an academic post.

William developed his heroine with assistance from Elizabeth, whom Marston believed to be a model of his era's unconventional, liberated woman. His heroine, like his spouse, was the ideal emancipated woman—one who fought prudery, prejudice, sexism, racism, and, as a superheroine, crime.

Now he needed another female for inspiration for his heroine's appearance. He found it in Olive Byrne. When William fell in love with his former student, he asked his wife if she would mind if they all lived together. She agreed to the polyamorous relationship. The Joneses they were not. William had two children with Elizabeth (Pete and Olive Ann), and two with Olive (Byrne and Donn).

For William's comic creation, he copied Olive's black hair and blue eyes. He drew on his character the heavy silver bracelets that Olive always wore on each wrist (he made them bullet deflectors). The fact that his comic character had a body that would do a supermodel proud and was six feet tall was sheer fantasy, as was her unique apparel. William outfitted her in high stiletto boots, hot pants decorated with stars, and a bustier that left a mere wisp to the imagination. In her hand was a magic lasso, which, when used to tie up villains, forced them to tell the truth (shades of the lie detector!). Instead of vaporizing her enemies, as her male superhero counterparts did, her magic lasso forced them to look into their own hearts, where she believed some remnant of good always resided. It's no wonder that she was named Wonder Woman.

The heroine made her dazzling debut in 1941 in *All Star Comics*; she was an Amazonian princess born in the testosterone-free Paradise Island, where she lived with a race of fellow Amazon women (Paradise Island indeed). She was described as "beautiful as Aphrodite, wise as Athena, swifter than Hermes, and stronger than Hercules." Her superheroine task was to help the Allies defeat the Axis powers. Marston wrote that she was to remain in America "to defend the last citadel of democracy, and of equal rights for women." In the course of her endeavors, she was often depicted in situations that simulated bondage, which makes one question how good a role model she was for girls. However, at times this situation did carry a positive message, as when she remarked when she escaped from restraints, "It's easy to break bonds if you know you can." It is admirable that the good doctor was an early proponent of women's rights.

Wonder Woman was initiated into the Justice League, its only female member to date. She was, however, a victim of her times after all, as she was given the job of secretary, though she could fight toe to toe (though clad in boots to her knees) with a certain man of steel.

Marston continued to create issues with Wonder Woman and lived with Elizabeth and Olive until his death from cancer at age fifty-four, in 1947. His two widows remained close, and Elizabeth supported Olive until her death in the 1980s. Elizabeth lived to be one hundred, spending her last three years in Connecticut with her son, Pete. Elizabeth worked on her autobiography as well as a history of the Magic Maiden. Elizabeth didn't do any actual physical writing, though; instead, she dictated "any damned thing I want." Her daughter, Olive Ann LaMotte, called her mother "a small package of dynamite."

As for the iconoclastic Amazing Amazon, she went on to help destroy European communism, all without acquiring a single gray hair or even a hint of cellulite. She remains the most powerful brunette in strapless spandex to educate three generations of action-loving superheroines.

If the Amazonian princess and Elizabeth Holloway Marston were both on the 1950s show *To Tell the Truth* and the host asked, "Will the real Wonder Woman please stand up?" there is no doubt that a certain feisty centenarian would rise, as she always did, to the occasion.

- In 1986, issue 329 was dedicated to Dr. Charles Moulton, a man who never existed. Dr. Marston had always written for DC Comics under that pseudonym. He came up with the name from his middle name, Moulton, and publisher Max Gaines' middle name, Charles.
- Dr. William Moulton Marston was inducted into the Comic Book Hall of Fame in 2006.
- Originally Marston named Wonder Woman "Suprema."

Eureka #23
(1943)

On occasion, eureka moments leave a very strange calling card. This was the case during World War II, when a naval officer, in an act of serendipity, witnessed an ordinary occurrence aboard a ship, which resulted in an immortal coil.

In 1943, a naval engineer in Philadelphia was assigned the task of keeping the instruments on ships stabilized, as movement made the panels difficult to read. He was experimenting with various springs when one of them fell to the floor. It was the metallurgical equivalent of Newton's apple. There were other men on board who saw the same thing but thought nothing of it. However, what Richard James saw led to his life's eureka moment: The spring could be used as a toy. The seemingly ordinary event would end up changing the man's destiny, as well as that of an industry.

That evening, when Richard returned home, he told his wife, Betty, about how the spring had bounced around the ship, as if it were imbibed with life. He said, "I think I can make a toy out of this." For the next two years, he worked on developing his product and assigned his wife to come up with a name. Although she had christened six children, she had never done so with an inanimate object and turned to a dictionary for inspiration. There she found a word of Swedish origin, which translated to "sleek or sinuous," and it stuck.

The couple borrowed $500 and produced four hundred of their product, on the gamble that their hunch would pay off. Richard churned out the coils, and Betty placed them in boxes. In 1945, on a cold, miserable November evening, Richard set up a display in Gimbels department store in Philadelphia. Fortunately, his space was at the end of the counter, so he was able to demonstrate his product's unique capability.

Betty, who accompanied him, said she was going for a coffee. When she was gone, she gave someone a dollar to buy a toy from her husband so that he would have at least one sale. When she returned, she realized her charitable gesture had been unnecessary. James was surrounded by hordes of people, all waving dollar bills. All four hundred were sold within ninety minutes. That snowy night, Slinky wielded the scepter.

Fame and fortune followed. The Jameses built a palatial home and adopted a lifestyle surpassing the scope of even their wildest daydreams. However, happiness proved elusive. In 1960, the toy story turned tabloid tale. Although Richard had a loving family, a lucrative factory, and a lavish lifestyle, he was not content. While other men satiate their midlife crises with fast cars and fast women, Richard chose an alternative route. He became enamored of a Bolivian religious cult, one to which he began to funnel most of his company's profits. Betty said of the sect, "I didn't know what it was. A lot of 'praise be, I'm saved.'" Richard began testifying at its revival meetings; Betty claimed Richard craved the attention he received while confessing to his sins. As it turned out, one of his sins included philandering. There ensued the domestic conversations that usually take place after such a declaration. The couple decided to stay together for the sake of their children. Betty was anxious to spare them her own unhappy childhood: Her mother had died when she was eight, and her father abandoned her soon after.

Not willing to merely finance the group, Richard decided to join them. He asked Betty to take their six children and accompany him to South America to join the cult. She refused. In 1960, James left his life for another. Betty was left holding the proverbial bag: one that consisted of being a single mother of six and owning a company faced with fast-encroaching bankruptcy. Other women in her position may have taken the route of sedatives, sanatoriums, or suicide. However, Betty James chose to adopt the Susan B. Anthony quotation: "Failure is not an option."

Betty assumed control of the factory, becoming its dynamic CEO. She employed the medium of television to advertise her product, and one of the most memorable of the commercial jingles became: "What walks down stairs, alone or in pairs, / and makes a slinkity sound?" She also introduced a whole new range of products based on the original one: Slinky Dog, Crazy Eyes (glasses with Slinky-extended fake eyeballs), Neon Slinky, Slinky Train, as well as a number of Slinky pets. Her hard work, which some people called luck, paid off, and the company became lucrative once more.

When asked about those difficult years, she responded, "When my husband left I wasn't going to sit down and say 'poor me.' You have to have a reason for being, and my family is mine. I kept going because I had no choice. I moved my family and I moved the factory, and even though I'd been working all along there was an awful lot I didn't know. I had children who had to be raised and educated. And they are all college graduates." When she was asked if she would ever remarry, her face wrinkled up, much as if she had encountered an unpleasant odor. "No! That wasn't even a passing thought. Anyway, who would want me with six children? My life has been so full. I'm perfectly happy." And, though she did not add this, financially very well off. Mrs. James does not make public her company's profits, but she did admit "business is phenomenal."

James Industries received a huge break in 1995, the year that Slinky celebrated its fiftieth anniversary (which it commemorated with a gold-plated model), when a redesigned Slinky Dog was chosen to star in *Toy Story*.

Another milestone was in 2001. In New York, a petite eighty-two-year-old woman, dressed in black, stepped off the elevator on the sixth floor of a Fifth Avenue building. One onlooker pointed her out as Betty James, adding, "I could tell by the diamonds on her fingers." She was in the National Toy Museum to be inducted into the Toy Hall of Fame, the forty-first person to be so honored. If the two men had known her story, they would have realized she had earned every one of those karats.

In 1998, Betty James sold her company, a move that ensured wealth for her family and the continuation of her beloved toy off*spring*. Although a spring falling off a table did not have the same impact as Newton's apple, Richard's eureka moment generated a toy that has become so much a part of Americana that it is on permanent display in the Smithsonian and was immortalized on a U.S. postage stamp. Quite an accomplishment for a toy that cannot talk and doesn't even need assembly. The toy industry, after more than half a century, has no plans to shake off this immortal coil.

Ever since a spring triggered a eureka moment during World War II, children and Slinkys have been as perfect a fit as a horse and carriage. The answer to the question as to whether or not Richard James ever achieved the salvation he so desperately sought died with him in Bolivia in 1974. However, the answer to the following riddle is one known to three past generations and many more to come: "What walks down stairs, alone or in pairs, / and makes a slinkity sound?"

- Although primarily used as a toy, Slinkys have served in a number of other functions. Soldiers in Vietnam threw Slinkys into trees and used them as radio antennae, and they have been used as physical therapy, to pick pecans, and in science classrooms.
- One of the early space missions took along a Slinky. They discovered that in space, it did not slink.
- Slinky made a guest appearance in John Waters' *Hairspray* and Jim Carrey's *Ace Ventura: When Nature Calls*.
- More than 300 million Slinkys have been sold. They would wrap around the world 126 times.

Eureka #24
(1950)

Shakespeare wrote, "We know what we are, but know not what we may be." Similarly, we may envision our projects in one way, only to be astounded with their ultimate outcome. This was the case with a Jewish athlete, whose inspired creation proved to have traveled far from its original eureka moment.

Gerard Blitz was born in Antwerp, a fourth-generation diamond merchant; however, the Blitzes cleaved water as much as they cut diamonds. Gerard's father and uncle were both European swimming champions, and he was a member of his country's water polo team. When the 1936 Olympics were held in Berlin, he refused to participate, believing that the Nazi-sponsored games were "inconsistent with the Olympic ideals of purity, political neutrality, solidarity, and liberty."

When the war broke out, Blitz was mobilized into the army and captured shortly after the German invasion of Belgium. He escaped and returned to Antwerp, where, in public, he worked as a swim instructor. However, his surreptitious job was to disseminate illegal political tracts denouncing the Nazis. His role was uncovered, and he was captured by the Germans at a swimming pool, though he was later released. His imprisonment, and the fact that his Jewish father (his mother was Catholic) soon had to wear a Star of David, led him to escape with his family to Switzerland, where he worked for the Belgian government in exile as a resistance fighter. In that capacity, he traveled throughout the Continent, where he developed a lifelong love of foreign locales.

After World War II, the Belgian government employed Blitz to look after his countrymen who had survived the Nazi concentration camps. In order to help nurture them back to health, Blitz created a chain of hotels in the Alps, centering around Chamonix.

When his work with the survivors was over, he went on a vacation with his son to Corsica. There he met two Frenchmen who said that they were enjoying the country's sandy beaches but had no idea what to do with themselves. Blitz stated that that "set me thinking," which led to his eureka moment: He could create a business of pleasure. Blitz felt that with his love of travel and his work with the concentration camp survivors, he would be able to devise what he called "the antidote to civilization."

When Blitz returned home, he decided to create an exotic retreat where weary Europeans could escape from the horrors of war. He envisioned it as a place where people could go for "mental and physical detoxification." In 1950, Gerard put up an advertisement in the Paris Metro: It was a poster of the sun, the sea, and his phone number. The response was overwhelming.

Blitz's vision for his getaway was a utopian destination founded on socialist principles, devoted to his twin passions of strengthening both the body and the spirit. His philosophy was to make a vacation a carefree one; in his holiday utopia, there would be no hunting for hotels, finding transportation, tipping, or tourist traps.

His location for his retreat was the Spanish island of Majorca. There he set up a vacation village, which, though in an idyllic setting, was extremely rustic: The accommodations were U.S. Army surplus tents supplied by fellow resistance fighter Gilbert Trigano, replete with hard cots. Other "amenities" included water from wells, communal showers, and pit toilets. Food was simple and guests were asked to help with chores, thereby contributing to the nonprofit association. The prevailing philosophy was one of egalitarian fun and community spirit, where vacationers would dine and exercise together, in the nature of an extended family. Everyone was expected to address one another by their first names, and the Spanish form *tu* rather than the formal *vous* was employed.

Blitz, as a die-hard anticapitalist, also sought to eradicate any class differences. Staff members, GOs (short for "gentils organisateuurs"), and GMs (short for "gentils membres") were all treated equally: They socialized, ate, cleaned, swam, and performed calisthenics and conga lines together on the beach. Blitz's maxim was "Down with class, down with castes."

Gerard also originated a novel approach for expenses: There would be one prepaid price for the whole package, as the handling of money would intrude on the willing suspension of reality. A few extras, such as drinks at the bar, were purchased with brightly colored bead necklaces, which were to emulate a carefree Polynesian life. Blitz christened his primitive paradise Club Méditerranée.

When the first batch of members returned to France, they did so singing the praises of the primitive paradise. Basking in the sun with strangers who had become friends helped allay the humiliation of the occupation: the roundup of the Jews, Hitler riding in his victory cavalcade through the Arc de Triomphe, the shaved heads of the collaborators. Club Med became as hot as its tropical island homes, and new exotic locales were added. Soon the army surplus tents gave way to thatched huts (with unlocked doors), and the simple fare morphed into sumptuous buffets. By the end of the 1960s, there were thirty-four Club Med villages in Europe, the United States, Israel, and French Polynesia. In them, even the most stressed of executives could revert to Peter Pan.

Gerard viewed his clubs as athletic ones; however, he also wanted his villages to cater to intellectual pursuits. With this in mind, he created in his retreats impressive libraries and record collections. In the evening, his more cerebral guests could attend poetry readings or forums on philosophical topics or classical music concerts. However, newspapers and radios were banned. His brochure, *Le Trident*, read, "Give your transistor a holiday too."

In 1954, Trigano went from supplying tents to the club to helping run it. He was the force behind the company's explosive growth and move to modernization. Perhaps in reaction to the new direction his brainchild had taken, Blitz turned to the discipline of yoga. He became the secretary and then head of the European Union of Yoga from 1974 until his passing in 1990. Trigano succeeded Blitz as president in 1963. However, as the founder, Blitz remained honorary president for the rest of his life. Together Blitz and Trigano had created a vacation where guests cried at their departure from the club, something they would not do when bidding adieu to a regular hotel.

Part of the secret to Club Med's power of endurance is its adaptability. In the unrepressed era of the 1970s, it became a magnet for those seeking not only sun and sea but sex. Hence, its moniker: Club Bed. Never had the unlocked doors become so convenient, and the ever-helpful GOs became willing attendants in a whole new way. The spirit of communal living envisioned by Gerard Blitz had taken on a life of its own.

A decade later, the hedonistic baby boomers of the '70s had transformed into the cost-conscious parents of the '80s, and Club Med adapted again to the times. It set up day-care centers where children would be entertained while parents grabbed some desperately needed adult time. Parts of some sites were designated for seniors; others to special-interest groups, such as Alcoholics Anonymous. Soon the only thing swinging was the circus trapeze, an integral part of the family villages.

Today *gentils membres* can choose from one hundred different exotic/erotic locales, where, for a time, they can pack up their troubles and leave reality behind. The current Club Med slogan is "Where Happiness Means the World." That, at least, is something the travel-loving Gerard Blitz would approve of.

Perhaps the secret of Club Méditerranée's success is that it has been able to reinvent itself as many times as Madonna:

from socialist tent camp to sex haven to high-thread-count sheets, from bohemian to bourgeois. In this ever-changing kaleidoscope, it reflects the many facets of Girard Blitz's life: diamond cutter, water polo champion, soldier, resistance fighter, Club Med visionary, and yoga devotee. However, the strand that still links the original concept of Club Med to its founder's initial eureka can be summarized in its founder's philosophy: that his Club Méditerranée would be "an antidote to civilization."

- Some 1.55 million people across the world are Club Med members.
- Club Med employs more than 20,000 people from eighty countries.
- In 1961, the Rothschild Group, led by Edmond de Rothschild, became the company's largest single stockholder.

Eureka #25
(1951)

I n 1950s Ireland, the serendipitous convergence of ale, birds, a knight with an animal name, and inquisitiveness led to a eureka moment that created the ultimate bible for those whose greatest pleasure lies in vindication.

The genesis of the epiphany began on a windy day in 1951 when South African–born Sir Hugh Beaver was on a hunting expedition on the coast of Ireland. Although he had bagged a number of birds, one eluded him—the golden plover. He attributed this not to his poor aim but to the fact that the golden plover must be the swiftest of Europe's game birds.

That evening, in Castleford House over bottles of ale, a spirited debate broke out over which bird was indeed the fastest. Sir Beaver maintained that it was the golden plover; his fellow hunters insisted it was the grouse. All parties were eager to say, "I told you so!" and they searched the host's extensive library for the answer. None was forthcoming.

Once back in England, where Hugh was the director of a brewery, he consulted a twenty-four-volume, $400 encyclopedia, trying such leads as birds, speed, velocity, and ornithology, but there was no mention of what he sought: a superlative regarding the fastest bird. This led to Hugh's eureka moment: There should be a definitive reference book to settle debates raging in the 73,000 pubs in Britain and in Ireland. Furthermore, he figured that those who would be able to respond with a resounding "I told you so!" would subliminally drink more of the beer from the makers of the publishers of the book that had proved him right.

He decided to act on his hunch and create such a volume that would shed light on questions such as the fastest, tallest, richest, and a myriad of other extremes. He would provide the guide to all of London's pubs. He had only to find a researcher up to such a daunting and unique task.

Sir Beaver mentioned the situation to his employee, Christopher Chataway, who was himself a holder of a five-thousand-meter record. Christopher suggested he contact Ross and Norris McWhirter, track fanatics who published a magazine, *Get to Your Marks*, as well as ran a fact-finding business.

Had the McWhirter twins been born in the Garden of Eden rather than in London, they would have wasted no time in biting the apple. At the age of eight, when most children are naturally inquisitive, the boys were curious to an extreme. When their over-questioned mother mentioned this to her husband, he responded that she should not provide them with the answers but encourage them to find out the information for themselves. Uncharacteristically for children, they delighted in their father's advice. While other British boys may have spent their time reading *Winnie-the-Pooh*, the McWhirters were only interested in absorbing facts. From an early age they had charted the deepest lakes, the longest tunnels, and the tallest buildings. To stimulate this pursuit, their father, an editor at the *London Daily Mail*, brought home 150 newspapers a week.

On Chataway's recommendation, the twins were invited to lunch in Sir Hugh's boardroom, replete with the firm's famous brew. The meal then evolved into a 1950s quiz bowl, with the directors trying to prove the McWhirter brothers not-know-enoughs. The questions, which included the world's heaviest living man (946 pounds), the longest line of chorus girls (Rockettes), and the most powerful lighthouse (France, 20 million candlepower), failed to elicit even the merest sweat from the fact-loving duo. When they were asked if they could find out information such as the world record for squatting on top of a pole, the brothers promptly responded that the distinction belonged to St. Simeon, a monk who stuck it out for more than thirty years atop a fifty-foot pillar near Qualat-Seman in Syria in the fifth century AD.

They did not, however, know offhand the top speed of the golden plover or of the fastest game bird. Nevertheless, Sir Hugh was otherwise impressed and formed a new subsidiary of his brewery: Guinness Superlatives Ltd.

In 1954, the McWhirters compiled a 197-page book with a green, beer-stain-resistant cover called *The Guinness Book of Records*; one thousand copies were printed and distributed to London's pubs for a mere seventy cents apiece. The book included the fastest game bird: neither the golden plover nor the grouse, but the wood pigeon.

Sir Hugh may have been proven wrong about his bird, but his eureka about his book proved correct. Surprisingly, the volume meant as a marketing ploy for beer rose to the top of the British nonfiction bestseller list by Christmas. The following year, it was distributed to the American market and sold 70,000 copies. The brothers, armed with their prodigious memories and endless thirst for knowledge, embarked on their lives' endeavor to continue to upgrade the book. They began a letter-writing campaign to government departments and university professors throughout the world. Tracking down superlatives had always been their passion; it now became their vocation. They worked tirelessly for Guinness, researching and verifying records, and putting their findings between the covers of what is arguably the most fun and fact-filled almanac in the world. The McWhirters became to trivia lovers in the 1950s what Robert "Believe It or Not" Ripley was to curiosity seekers in the 1930s. In the world according to Guinness, superlatives have existed ever since the Big Bang, but it took a Beaver and a bet on the coast of Ireland to transform them into a green-covered volume.

One of the easiest answers was to the question, Who left the largest Irish will? It was for £13,486,146, left by the first Earl of Iveagh, who, born with the surname Guinness, went on to create a family fortune founded on ale. In deference to their publisher, the McWhirters made no mention of the Guinness family, although they could have mentioned that the family also held the record for the largest brewery in Europe and the most beer, ale, and stout exports.

Tragically, the brothers, who worshipped the same god as Doctor Faustus, likewise had to pay a horrific price. In 1975, after Ross McWhirter's friend John Gouriet failed to persuade Home Secretary Roy Jenkins to offer a reward for information leading to a conviction for several high-profile bombings in England, which had been carried out by the Irish Republican Army, Ross took matters into his own hands and put up £50,000 in reward money. He also advocated for stronger restrictions on the Irish community in Britain. In retaliation, three weeks later, two members of the IRA, both of whom were also members of what became known as the Balcombe Street Gang, shot him at close range in the head and chest while he stood on his doorstep. The men responsible were arrested two weeks later and sentenced to life in prison. They served twenty-two years but were released as part of the peace agreement for Northern Ireland.

Norris said of his brother's assassination that it felt like an amputation; grief-stricken, he vowed to "shoulder on." Norris continued to edit the book until the Guinness Brewery pushed him out in 1986. That same year, he launched an unsuccessful defamation case against the Independent Broadcasting Authority for the TV show *Spitting Image*. He was indignant because they had inserted a subliminal image of McWhirter's face imposed on the body of a naked woman.

Failure to bag a golden plover resulted in a multimillion-dollar-a-year enterprise and made a company, once known only for its frothy dark beer, a favorite household book. Since its inception half a century ago, the company's scribes have chronicled statistics from the sublime to the ridiculous. Under the category of bestselling books, the 2005 golden anniversary edition states, "Excluding non-copyright works such as the Bible and the Koran, the world's all-time bestselling book is the *Guinness World Records*, proved by cumulative sales exceeding 100 million." For a time, the McWhirter twins were the bestselling nonfiction authors in the world.

Under the McWhirter twins, the book became much more than a compilation of unusual superlatives. Its true spirit was about challenge, about people pushing themselves to their utmost to achieve acclaim both in the eyes of the world and in their own. The successful book, which began with a brew and a bet, has a universal appeal because it speaks to our unquenchable thirst for challenge—against the elements and against oneself.

- The rules are stringent about inclusion in the book. It currently requires video evidence, still photos, newspaper clippings, and testimonials. Few meet the standards. One American, who had played a church organ for thirty hours but could not furnish proof, complained to the queen.
- Currently the task of charting the world's superlatives rests with those employed in an eighth-floor suite of offices in an ultra-modern glass building in central London. Nine full-time researchers handle 60,000 inquiries a year from would-be record breakers. Whenever possible, they are sent on location to investigate: to China (Largest Golf Club), to India (Longest Dance Party), and to Mexico (Largest Burrito). Approximately 30,000 records are set each year.
- In 2005, Guinness designated November 9 as International Guinness World Records Day to encourage the breaking of world records. In 2006, 100,000 people in more than ten countries participated.

- Guinness World Records now has museums in tourist areas from Niagara Falls to Los Angeles. Guinness television programs air in more than eighty-five countries. Its website gets 14 million hits a month, and its latest edition has sold 3 million copies in twenty-three languages.

Eureka #26
(1957)

Stories that begin with "Once upon a time" are usually rife with dysfunctional families. Unfortunately, dysfunction is not just fodder for fairy tales. One modern-day Brooklyn family's breakdown was caused by its patriarch's eureka, which, although it brought fame and fortune, led to tragedy, enacted against a backdrop of pink.

Benjamin Eisenstadt, the son of Russian Jewish immigrants, was eight years old when his mother sent him to give his father a change of clothes because he was in the hospital. On his arrival, a nun told him that his father was with Jesus; Ben at first assumed Jesus was one of the Hispanic workers who labored in his tenement.

His father's death left the family even more poverty-stricken, and Ben was pawned off to a series of relatives. In a sense, the abandonment proved positive: He was free to invent himself in his own image.

When Ben was twenty-five, he married Pessie Gellman, whose father had left Russia to escape its pogroms. When she began school, she could only speak Yiddish, and suffered from the stigma of being "the only Jew present." To be more anglicized, she changed her name to Bessie, then Betty.

After Ben and Betty were married, they worked at the Gellman Diner, which fed the old Ebbets Field throng after games and had the dubious distinction of being the hangout of a group of tough Jews known as Murder Incorporated. When they had word that a cop was coming, they would drop their weapons into Betty's apron, and she would hide them in the onion bin.

The couple had four children: Marvin, Gladys, Ellen, and Ira. During the war, the couple opened a restaurant on Cumberland Street, across from the Brooklyn Navy Yard. World War II turned the area into a boomtown, and the couple bought a home in Flatbush, where their affluence made them the Lords of Flatbush. The wealth helped satisfy Betty's eternal thirst for money; her oft-repeated plea was, "If I just had a lump sum . . ." Money was insurance her family would be able to pay off the border guards if Jewish people had to flee a country once more.

After the war, when the navy depot closed, the area became a ghost town, and the diner closed. As a child, Ben had lived with an uncle who had owned a teabag-packing business, and Ben turned the Cumberland Diner into the Cumberland Packing Company. Unable to compete with Tetley or Lipton, Ben was under extreme financial pressure. He had a wife and four children, as well as two newly immigrated in-laws to support. After he sold his eatery's fixtures, Ben had just enough cash to purchase a teabag-making machine and a rare meal out with Betty.

In 1947, Ben and Betty went for lunch at a deli, where they bemoaned the fiasco of their factory. Little did they realize when the waitress put down their mugs of tea that she was, symbolically, offering the Eisenstadts a kingdom—a pink one. Betty went to sweeten her beverage and reached for the sugar. At that time, sugar came either in bowls on the table, which were a haven for flies and dirty spoons, or in heavy glass dispensers, whose openings often clogged. As Betty flipped over the glass dispenser, she banged it to coax out the stubborn white granules. This led to an epiphany: Instead of packaging tea, Ben could package sugar. This would get rid of the sugar bowls and sugar dispensers and replace it with something America would understand: a disposable packet. Ecstatic, Ben approached Domino Sugar with his idea; they never got back to him but began producing the packets themselves. As Ben had not taken out a patent, he was convinced they had hijacked his invention.

Occasionally, lightning strikes twice, and the same holds true of eureka moments. A few years later, Ben was approached by a company requesting that his factory try producing a packaged sugar substitute as an aid for diabetics. However, when Ben and his son Marvin came up with the product, the company had dropped the project. Undeterred, Ben decided to market it to hospitals on his own—this time with a patent. He came up with the name Sweet'N Low from a Tennyson poem, "The Princess: Sweet and Low," which had become the lyrics to an 1863 song Ben had listened to as a boy. It was also a tribute to Betty, his own princess. They packaged it in bright pink, to distinguish it from Domino's white one, and the logo was a blue treble clef, in allusion to the song.

To their astonishment, the demand for Sweet'N Low was insatiable. Hospitals reported that the substitute was being pilfered, not just by diabetics but by those fighting the battle of the bulge, which led to Ben's next eureka: tapping into the country's diet obsession. Soon his packets had replaced not just old-fashioned sugar dispensers but even sugar itself.

And though the family fortune was built on the Sweet'N Low formula, so was its breakdown. It would serve to turn the life of the middle-class family into a modern soap-opera saga of the super-rich.

Sweet'N Low promised sweetness without guilt, and soon 50 million pink packages were being produced each day, generating millions of dollars. However, Ben's son Marvin, known as "Marvelous," was charged with criminal conspiracy for making illegal campaign contributions to Senator Alfonse D'Amato (who had ties to a crime family) so that he would not approve a ban on the artificial sweeter, which had gone into effect when rats died after being injected with it. The outcome of the trial was that Marvelous received a one-year probation, and Cumberland was fined over $2 million.

At home, Gladys, after contracting psoriasis as a young woman, did not leave the Flatbush family home for thirty years. Ira became eccentric, living with dozens of cats.

Ellen, after meeting Herb Cohen, told her father that she had met the man she wanted to marry. In response, Ben pointed to his eyes, his heart, and his crotch and then asked his daughter, "Do you love him here, here, or here?" When she replied that she loved him in all three places, he threw his Brooklyn princess a lavish wedding and walked down the aisle to give her away.

However, what mainly led to the schism in the family was when Ben, at age eighty-nine, was hospitalized for a heart condition, which led to his death. (His obituary in the *New York Times* called him "a sweetener of lives.") The problems originated with Ellen's recommendation of an eminent cardiologist. With Ben's death, Betty, bereft at losing her prince and fueled by a vindictive house-bound Gladys, blamed Ellen. At her own demise, her will stipulated, "I hereby record that I have made no provision under this WILL for my daughter ELLEN and any of ELLEN'S issue for reasons I deem sufficient." Her will, like many other documents that begin with the fateful words, "I, being of sound mind" irrevocably splintered the family.

Ellen and Herb's son Rich has written a tell-all memoir, *Sweet and Low: A Family Story*, which uncovers the bitterness inherent in the sweetener giant. In his book he publicly dusts off his family skeletons. He writes how Uncle Marvelous could have lived up to his moniker by sharing his fortune with his sister. Aunt Gladys, who never leaves her home and therefore certainly does not need millions, could have made provisions, if not for her sister, at least for her nephew and nieces. Similarly, the childless Uncle Ira could have shared the wealth that the sugar substitute built. After all, even if each of his dozen cats live out each of their nine lives, there would still be a surplus of green.

Most people who have had their birthright of millions of dollars snatched from them would have been devastated. However, Rich Cohen explains that, like his grandfather, it left him free to invent himself. Perhaps what helped him take the latter path was the love of his mother and his siblings, as shown in *Sweet and Low*'s dedication: "To Ellen and her issue." What comes across even stronger than Cohen's understandable anger is his indomitable spirit.

Reading Rich's saga of his Brooklyn family is akin to sitting in an amphitheater watching a Greek tragedy. It can be enjoyed on one level as the triumphs and tribulations of the wealthy, and on another level as the history of an industry. However, its chief satisfaction stems from the realization that no matter how dysfunctional one's family is, one can still reinvent oneself and prevail.

- Maimonides Medical Center has the Eisenstadt Administration Building in honor of its benefactors.
- U.S. trademark #1,000,000 was given to Brooklyn's Cumberland Packing Company.
- The company today employs four hundred people and is still on the original site of Ben's diner. There are also plants in England, India, Israel, and Canada.
- For Sweet'N Low's fiftieth anniversary, the Pink Panther and Regis Philbin, replete with pink bow tie and pink handkerchief, advertised the product on its packaging for the commemorative year.

Eureka #27
(1959)

In the early 1900s, thousands of self-imposed exiles were processed at Ellis Island; they came to escape prosecution and with the hope that life would be better in America. Unfortunately, without mastering the language or a U.S. education, their dreams were mainly relegated to the realm of sleep. However, because of a eureka moment, one of these newcomers' children would achieve a success beyond her parents' wildest dreams.

Ruth Moskowic, the youngest of ten children, was a first-generation American; her parents had escaped from anti-Semitic Poland. At age sixteen, she met Isadore Elliot Handler at a B'nai B'rith dance in Denver. Ruth and Elliott (she preferred his middle name) married and moved to Los Angeles, taking with them only their love for each other—they would have to make their way from the bottom up.

In 1942, the Handlers started a company with Harold Matson. They christened it by combining Matson and Elliot; thus, Mattel was born. They started off by making doll furniture in their apartment's garage; however, they later switched to toys. Mattel was catapulted to fame when Ruth came up with the novel idea of advertising on the new medium of television. They purchased a year's exclusive rights to advertise on ABC's *Mickey Mouse Club*. Ruth's comment about her brainchild was not an exaggeration: "I am a marketing genius."

The Handlers had two children, daughter Barbara and son Kenneth; unlike other '50s women, Ruth continued to work outside the home. One day Ruth observed the preteen Barbara playing with paper dolls by assigning them adult roles. This led to Ruth's eureka moment: The market was ready for a grown-up doll, specifically one with breasts. Eagerly she explained her vision to Elliot and Harold, but they thought it was not marketable.

In the mid-1950s, on a family trip to Lucerne, Switzerland, Ruth came across an adult doll made in Germany called Bild Lilli. The toy was based on a popular character featured in a comic strip for the newspaper *Die Bild-Zeitung*. In the comic, Bild Lilli's life philosophy was embodied by statements such as, "I could do without balding old men but my budget couldn't," and, "The sunrise is so beautiful that I always stay late at the nightclub to see it!" Bild Lilli was marketed with the phrase that her wardrobe would make her "the star of every bar."

Ruth gave a doll to her daughter and decided to make Bild Lilli available, in a transformed state, in the United States. Of course, it must remain a matter of conjecture why a mother would buy a German sex doll for her preteen daughter and then try to sell it to American children, but whatever the cause, the result was that Ruth Handler became a billionaire.

Because she was targeting a young audience, she transformed Bild Lilli, who resembled a disheveled Marlene Dietrich, into a less sexual model. Ruth hired Jack Ryan, a former engineer for the Pentagon, to help revamp the doll's image, transforming her from a German streetwalker into a sultry American teenager. Ruth christened the doll Barbie, after her daughter's nickname.

In show-and-tell fashion, Ruth took her product to her husband, but Elliot and all of the other male executives were not enthusiastic. They felt the tried-and-true dolls, such as Betsy Wetsy, were the only ones children would relate to. Moreover, they felt that Barbie was far too sexual, as she had breasts, heavy black eyeliner, black stilettos, and a come-hither expression. However, Mattel was finally persuaded, and on March 9, 1959 (Barbie's official birthday), they took her to the American Toy Fair in New York City.

Although mothers were not happy with the blond bombshell, their daughters were ecstatic. Within the first year, 352,000 were sold at $3 each. Currently, more than a billion have been sold, at prices far exceeding the original. The anatomically incorrect molded statuette, with the Scarlett O'Hara waist, became an American icon. Ruth Handler later said in the *New York Times* of her eureka moment, "Every little girl needed a doll through which to project herself into her dream of a future. If she was going to do role playing of what she would be like when she was 16 or 17, it was a little stupid to play with a doll that had a flat chest. So I gave it beautiful breasts."

In 1950s America, it was necessary for the Handlers to create a significant other for Barbie, as females were considered failures without a male. Ruth named him Ken after her son, Kenneth. He was advertised with the slogan, "He's a doll!" Because of the furor that had erupted over Barbie's measurements, they deliberated on how anatomically correct Ken should be. To be on the safe side, the Handlers decided Ken should have underwear permanently molded to his body. His official name was Ken Carson, and when he met Barbie, it was love at first sight. Ironically, though Barbie possesses innumerable wedding gowns, she has never wed her long-time boy toy.

Although for most of her life, Barbie's world has been a rose-strewn runway, even into the most charmed, pink-hued existence some rain must fall. The most traumatic was her split, in February 2004, from Ken, after forty-three years of coupledom. The end of the perfect plastic couple's relationship was huge grist for the gossip mill. The catalyst for their break-up was because Barbie dumped Ken for Californian boogie boarder Blaine. The vice president of marketing at Mattel stated that Barbie and Ken "feel it's time to spend some quality time apart." Happily, after two years, they reconciled.

During the breakup, the Bratz dolls started to muscle into Barbie's territory. While she was reeling from this, there cropped up a host of parodies, such as Postal Worker Barbie, complete with a machine gun; Trailer Trash Barbie, complete with dangling cigarette; and Bondage Barbie, complete with S&M accessories. The real Barbie's résumé, however, has included ninety careers.

Prior to these challenges, our heroine was the victim of an American group, the BLO (the Barbie Liberation Organization). Feminists, already infuriated with Barbie's philosophy of

"Life is fantastic when you're plastic" and with her anorexic body, felt the 1989 Teen Talk Barbie was the proverbial last straw. This model uttered phrases such as "Math is hard!" In retaliation, they decided to do some gender bending. The toy terrorists broke into stores at night and performed corrective surgery: They exchanged the voice boxes of the Barbies with the voice boxes of G.I. Joes. One can only imagine the faces of the little girls when their Barbie uttered in a deep growl, "Eat lead, Cobra!" Similarly, little boys heard their testosterone-free Joes sighing, "Ken is such a dream."

Love her or hate her, Barbara Millicent Roberts is here to stay. And no matter what future slings and arrows come her way, we can rest assured she will always land on her feet, shod in stylish, sexy stilettos.

At age fifty-four, Ruth Handler was diagnosed with breast cancer. Inspired by the difficulty of finding a good breast pros-thesis, she decided to make her own, and founded her com-pany Nearly Me. In talking about her two careers, Mrs. Handler said, "I've lived my life from breast to breast." She also became a well-traveled advocate for early detection of breast cancer at a time when there was little public discussion of the disease. At times during these years she opened her blouse at interviews and asked reporters or photographers to feel her breasts to determine which was real.

Because of her eureka moment, the daughter of immi-grants created an icon that became one of the pillars of Americana.

- The 1965 Slumber Party Barbie came with a book on how to lose weight with the advice, "Don't eat."

- Mattel claims that three Barbie dolls are sold every second; more than 1 billion have been sold. Ninety percent of all American girls have owned at least one Barbie. If every Barbie doll ever manufactured were laid end to end, they would circle the earth three and a half times.
- In 1985, Andy Warhol painted Barbie.
- In 2003, Saudi Arabia outlawed the sale of Barbie dolls on the principle that Barbie does not conform to the ideals of Islam. They stated, "Jewish Barbie dolls, with their revealing clothes and shameful postures, accessories, and tools, are a symbol of decadence to the perverted West. Let us beware of her dangers and be careful." In response, the Middle Eastern countries created an alternative doll called Fulla, who is dressed in Islamic fashion.
- Barbie didn't have a belly button until 2000.
- A typical American girl owns eight Barbie dolls.

Eureka #28
(1960)

One of the world's most familiar pictorial maxims is the image of the three wise monkeys that embody the principle of "see no evil, speak no evil, hear no evil." In the 1960s, a man in a bowler hat had a eureka that was to do far more than merely closing one's eyes, mouth, and ears to evil.

The Benensons were a Russian Jewish family whose patriarch, Grigori, earned a fortune under the tsar from banking and oil. Due to their wealth and their religion, they were forced to flee during the communist revolution. The family escaped to London, where Flora Benenson married Harold Solomon, a brigadier general in World War I. Their union resulted in the birth of their only child, Peter.

In 1920, Harold was attached to the high commissioner in Palestine, and so he moved the family there, which made Flora extremely happy, as she was an ardent Zionist. Three years later, Peter was devastated when his father suffered a serious riding accident and was confined to a wheelchair.

When the family returned to London, Harold and Flora's marriage, never a happy one, disintegrated. Harold passed away in Switzerland, the day before Peter's ninth birthday. His son was inconsolable, and it contributed to lifelong depression.

Flora was left to raise her son alone; later, in her autobiography, she confessed that she was an unsatisfactory mother. However, although Peter may not have grown up in a happy home, his mother was to serve as his role model. Flora played a key part in improving customer conditions at Marks & Spencer stores in the United Kingdom. In 1930, over dinner with Simon Marks, she bewailed the company's salary policy. Her stinging comment was, "It's firms like Marks & Spencer that give Jews a bad name." Marks responded by putting Flora Solomon in charge of staff welfare.

At home, she hired W. H. Auden as Peter's tutor. However, Auden, when not tutoring, was continuing his relationship with a male lover in their Kensington home. Flora packed Peter off to Eton, where he proved he was indeed Flora's son. After observing hunger marchers from South Wales, he became a socialist. A complaint he made to the headmaster regarding the poor quality of food prompted the irate principal to write Flora of her son's "revolutionary tendencies." The epistle must have met maternal approbation rather than the expected ire.

Peter organized support for the Spanish Republican government as it fought the military uprising against the dictator Franco, and financially adopted a Spanish baby. He also spearheaded a movement and raised £4,000 to bring two young German Jewish teenagers to school in Britain in 1939. It was while he was at Eton that he rejected his Judaism and converted to Roman Catholicism. Another change was his name. When his grandfather died, Peter acceded to his wish that he adopt his surname, and thus Peter Solomon became Peter Benenson.

Post-graduation, Peter entered Oxford, but his studies were interrupted when he joined the army in its Nazi code-breaking division. At this time, he married Margaret Anderson, with whom he had two daughters. The marriage was not to last, but he proved himself the loving parent his mother had not been.

Although he was ostensibly the picture of bourgeois conformity, Peter did not abandon his earlier advocacy for social justice. In the early 1950s, he went to Spain as the observer of the trials of trade unionists and was shocked by Generalissimo Franco's courts and prisons. He also journeyed to Hungary to participate in its uprising and subsequent trials, and to South Africa where a major "treason trial" was to take place. These trips, however, were merely the preface to his greatest act.

One day, on his way to work as a lawyer, Peter Benenson sat in the London Underground, bowler hat on head, attaché case at his side, reading the *Daily Telegraph*, when a small article caught his eye. It dealt with two teenage students in Portugal who had raised their glasses in a tipsy toast to liberty in a Lisbon café. The reigning dictator had outlawed such expressions, and the boys were sentenced to seven years imprisonment. Infuriated at the trammeling of freedom of speech and incensed at their punishment, Benenson left the Underground at Trafalgar Square with the intent to protest at the Portuguese embassy.

However, instead, feeling he would receive more guidance in a house of worship than in a political arena, he went to the church of St. Martin-in-the-Fields, the Christopher Wren house of worship. It was there he had his eureka moment: He decided to galvanize support for those victimized by repressive regimes. His means to achieve this end was a public appeal to write letters to liberate the unjustly imprisoned.

A few weeks later, the front page of the *Observer* carried an impassioned editorial by Peter titled "The Forgotten Prisoners," which was a call to emotional arms to put pressure on dictatorships actively imprisoning what he termed "prisoners of conscience." It concluded with the statement, "Governments are prepared to follow only where public opinion leads. Pressure of opinion 100 years ago brought about the emancipation of the slaves. It is now for man to insist upon the same freedom for his mind as he has won for his body." Books have often reformed the world; this time the task was accomplished by a newspaper.

Newspapers as diverse as the *New York Herald Tribune*, *Die Welt*, and the *Statesman of India* reprinted Peter's editorial, and it had a galvanizing effect on like-minded people. Rather than the handful of responses Peter anticipated, there were thousands. The newspaper article had found a responsive chord with those wanting to reignite the largely ignored 1948 Universal Declaration of Human Rights. Encouraged, Peter organized a twelve-month letter-writing campaign.

A few months later, a meeting of supporters, backed by a growing number of devotees from Belgium, Britain, France, Germany, Ireland, Switzerland, and the United States, decided to establish "a permanent international movement in defense of freedom of opinion and religion." Amnesty International was born. It was to become a significant force in beating swords into plowshares.

For its symbol, members adopted a design by the British artist Diana Redhouse. It was an apt metaphor for Amnesty: a candle encircled by barbed wire. Referring to the image, Benenson said, "Once the concentration camps and the hell-holes of the world were in darkness. Now they are lit by the light of the Amnesty candle; the candle in barbed wire. When I first lit the Amnesty candle, I had in mind the old Chinese proverb: 'Better light a candle than curse the darkness.'" The latter phrase became the motto of his human rights organization. The budget, funded by donations, was so small that it was often worked out on a cigarette package while members congregated at a pub. However, the force of the idea was contagious, and soon branches sprang up in several countries.

The official birth of Amnesty International took place in Luxembourg in 1961, presided over by Benenson. Sixteen years later, in recognition of its role in making the world a more humane place, Amnesty International was awarded the Nobel Peace Prize. However, the organization was represented by the Swedish chairman rather than its founder. This was because Peter never wanted any recognition. He expressed this sentiment when he stated that the ultimate objective of his organization "is to close for business." It was his unassuming nature that made him decline all offers of knighthood, saying that if they truly wished to honor his work, they should clean up their own backyard first. He then set out a litany of human-rights violations in which the British government was complicit. Not only did Benenson demonstrate by his own actions the power of one to change the world, but he did so with the desire that no personal laurels crown his brow.

In the half century since it was founded, Amnesty International has grown to a membership of 2 million people, with branches in more than 160 countries. Unfortunately, there has never been a shortage of work for the organization, as they react to human rights violations across the globe: South Africa, Chile, Iraq, Burma, Rwanda, Somalia, the former Yugoslavia, Latin America, Romania, Russia, and countless other regimes where dictators are committed to the suppression of individual freedom. On the twentieth anniversary of Amnesty International, Peter lit a candle in St. Martin-in-the-Fields church and said, "I have lit this candle, in the words of Shakespeare, 'against oblivion' so that the forgotten prisoners should always be remembered. We work in Amnesty against oblivion." Benenson was committed to the belief that ordinary people could bring about extraordinary change.

Sadly, even an organization built on the pillar of idealism can show cracks. In 1966, Amnesty International faced an internal crisis when Benenson made allegations of improper conduct against other members of the organization. An inquiry was set up in Elsinore in Denmark. When his accusations were rejected, Benenson, in protest, resigned as president and devoted his days to farming, writing, and prayer.

When his marriage to Margaret ended, he wed Susan Booth, who worked at an Oxford museum. They ended up separating but reconciled when he was in his sixties. In his later years, Peter was injured in a serious motor accident, which was compounded by celiac disease and bipolar condition. Fortunately, his pain was abated by visits from his children, grandchildren, and numerous friends. Surrounded by them and the admiration of a grateful world, the man who fought for the forgotten passed away from pneumonia in Oxford at age eighty-three.

Although Peter Benenson is departed, the candle he lit continues to shine, a ray of light that gives hope in the world's darkest places. It was this man in a bowler hat, sitting in London's Tube reading a newspaper, whose eureka struck a match to the conscience of the world.

- Benenson was the chairman of the Association of Christians Against Torture. He also was engaged in helping orphans of Ceauşescu's Romania.
- In 1961, Penguin published Peter's book *Persecution*, which outlined the stories of nine prisoners of conscience.
- In 1967, Amnesty International was awarded consultative status with Unesco.
- In 1979, Amnesty International published a list of 2,665 people known to have "disappeared" in Argentina following the military coup of Jorge Rafael Videla.

Eureka #29

(1963)

The word "cookies" evokes memories: To some, it awakens an image of a blue-furred *Sesame Street* dweller; to others, brown-tunic wearing girls. However, to one woman, it led to a eureka moment, and the way her cookie crumbled made her the queen of Queens.

Jean Slutsky was born into a Jewish family in Brooklyn. Her father drove a taxi and her mother worked as a manicurist. She explained that being a manicurist was about more than doing nails; it was about holding hands, hearing stories, and helping. Unfortunately, from a young age Jean was burdened with a problem (other than her surname) when she mushroomed into an overweight child. Jean recalled of her pudgy years, "I don't really remember, but I'm positive that whenever I cried, my mother gave me something to eat."

Jean later dated a man whom she met at a diner. She recalls, "I was sitting at a luncheonette. Eating. And he was sitting next to me. Eating. We fell in love and we loved to eat. We knew every restaurant in Queens that did second helpings.

We'd eat anything that didn't move." Marty Nidetch and Jean married and moved to Queens, where he worked as a bus driver. Jean became a stay-at-home mother, who made pocket money delivering eggs door to door.

With time the pounds piled up, and eventually Jean had to support 214 pounds. In her autobiography, she described herself as "an overweight woman, married to an overweight husband, surrounded by overweight friends with a fat poodle." She was the sixties version of a "desperate housewife." She reached her breaking point in a supermarket.

While shopping for food (Jean's Achilles' heel was chocolate cookies), an acquaintance asked when she was due. Humiliated, Nidetch took two buses and a subway and attended a free weekly workshop sponsored by New York City called the Obesity Clinic, which featured a diet regimen by Dr. Norman Jolliffe. When she arrived, the participants were mainly wearing coats and sunglasses. She adopted its tenets as her eating bible. However, what really helped more than the menu was the camaraderie from others attending the workshop. Soon she was dropping pounds faster than a bride-to-be.

However, despite her success, she weakened under the siren's lure of chocolate cookies. Jean did not feel comfortable talking to the thin woman who ran the clinic because she could not understand why someone desperate to lose weight would cheat. In desperation, she invited six overweight friends over to help her flagging resolve. Her despair echoed her friends' own. After all, this was the decade when Twiggy dominated the runway. They empathized and encouraged; they also shared their own "Frankensteins," as Jean called their collective food obsessions.

Their sisterhood of solidarity led to Jean's eureka moment: The battle of the bulge was best fought collectively. With her newfound knowledge that mutual support was the key, the friends started meeting weekly at the Nidetch home. As they all lost weight (including Marty, who lost seventy pounds, and Jean's mother, who lost fifty-seven), word spread and soon Jean was squeezing forty people into her small apartment. Nidetch recalls, "We weren't going to blame our genes, our hormones, or our mothers anymore." This novel approach was to ultimately launch a thousand self-help movements.

Because of the space problem, Jean drove her Studebaker to other homes; one of them belonged to Albert and Felice Lippert, whose sons described them as "two beach balls." When Albert lost forty pounds and Felice lost fifty, they were converts. It was on one of these visits that Albert had his business epiphany: He realized Jean's plan had the seed of a business venture. On the Lipperts' kitchen table, in May 1963, a partnership agreement was set up between the two couples: They christened it Weight Watchers. Lippert recalls, "We did it almost as a lark. We told each other we'd been 'living off the fat of the land' and that we deserved to win the 'Nobelly Prize.'"

The four cofounders opened their business on the floor above a movie theater in Queens; Albert had to sign the lease because Jean, as a woman, could not. They charged for admission the same price as a movie ticket: $2. They optimistically set up fifty chairs and were astonished when four hundred people queued up. Jean spent the entire day addressing the overwhelming despair of the overweight. She then outlined her battle strategy. She explained, "Compulsive eating is an emotional problem and we use an emotional approach to its solution. To me, this is just plain common sense." However, common sense was apparently not that common, for no one had used that approach before. Of that initial meeting, Jean recalled stuffing more money into her bag than she had ever seen in her life.

Nidetch started holding meetings three times a day, seven days a week. Not able to keep up the brutal pace, Al suggested that she pick key people who had been through her program to expand it. Weight Watchers caught on like the proverbial wildfire. It became the evangelical movement of Queens. Through franchises, what worked in Jean's cramped apartment began working from New York to California, from Australia to Brazil.

However, Marty was not thrilled that the person he had married seemed to be turning into someone else. On one occasion he asked her, "When is this going to be over? I liked you better when you sold eggs." Her mother, not comfortable with her daughter's frequent absences, also pleaded with her to stop and asked her, "Why can't you be a manicurist like me?" However, Jean had found her calling, and there was no turning back.

In 1978, the company reached annual sales of $50 million, with 102 franchises in the United States, Canada, Great Britain, Israel, and Puerto Rico. The ever-entrepreneurial Al then moved on to merchandising to supermarkets, opening summer camps for overweight children, and publishing *Weight Watchers* magazine.

Despite the runaway success, Jean never lost her modesty. She said when given accolades, "I'm just an ex-fat lady who had a good idea one day." She also never lost her integrity. In

South Africa, she aborted her inspirational talk when she noticed a sign: "No Blacks." She refused to enter. She said, "I don't look at someone's skin. I don't care what their religion is. All I care about is what they ate for breakfast, what they ate for lunch."

At this juncture, Jean had shed seventy pounds—and Marty. Her jet-set lifestyle had taken its toll on her twenty-four-year marriage, although she had given it some of the thinnest years of her life. She was flying first-class all over the world, dressed in fur coats and sling-back heels, accompanied by security guards. A picture of her in a slinky white dress was used to promote tins of Weight Watchers fish. She relished the spotlight, a place where her steadfastly blue-collar husband never felt comfortable. Although she had bought Marty his own bus company, the venture was not successful; he preferred just to be the man behind the wheel.

With characteristic chutzpah, Jean rebounded and went on to date Fred Astaire. There was even a shipboard romance with an Italian bass player whom she met on a cruise ship and married within a week. She says, "I called him the Italian stallion but it wasn't to last. We never fought, but we never talked either." She relocated to Brentwood, California, where she was known as Lean Jean.

During Weight Watchers' tenth anniversary at Madison Square Garden in New York City, with Bob Hope in attendance, Jean spoke until 1:30 a.m., regaling her audience with inspiring stories of weight loss and life success. A great motivational speaker, her tagline is "It's choice—not chance—that determines your destiny."

Currently Jean Nidetch, the queen of dieting from Queens,

lives in a retirement community in Florida. With her bleached-blond hair and sparkly clothes, she's every bit the Florida Golden Girl. She said, "You know, many people say to me, it's difficult to be in my program. But, I say, do you see this hair? It's blond. I'm eighty-four. Do you think I was born with this color? It's *hard*. I have to get to the beauty parlor; it's expensive, and sometimes, it burns my scalp. You have to work at it! Who said I have to be blond? Not God! I want to be blond. And sometimes it's not easy."

The story of a New York cabbie's daughter, Jean Slutsky, who went from a poor, overweight girl to a wealthy and svelte woman, is the stuff of Hollywood romance. Her empire led to the thinning of America. However, it accomplished this not just with a diet regiment but because Jean understood that helping people lose weight was also "about holding hands, hearing stories, and helping." Thus, in a fashion, she had followed in her mother's footsteps after all. If only this were the way all our cookies (chocolate and otherwise) would crumble...

- At Weight Watchers' ten-year birthday event at Madison Square Garden, the New York State Department renamed Times Square "Weight Watchers Square" for the week.
- Nidetch stipulated that all Weight Watchers franchise holders must have once been overweight and be willing to display "before" pictures from their XXL days.
- The Weight Watchers cookbook made it to the bestsellers list and sold 1.5 million copies.
- The H.J. Heinz Co. purchased Weight Watchers for $100 million.

Eureka #30
(1963)

Pink has been adopted as the signature color for a number of celebrities: Barbie, Hello Kitty, and *Grease*'s Pink Ladies, among others. However, there was one woman who predated all of these bright-hued females, and her relationship with pink left her rolling in green.

Mary Kathlyn Wagner was born in rural Hotwells, Texas, allegedly in 1916. Clinging to the philosophy that "a lady never reveals her age," Mary Kathlyn, although she would eventually publicize many private aspects of her life, never revealed the true date of her entrance into the world.

Her mother, Lula, the family breadwinner, worked as a waitress from 5 a.m. to 9 p.m. seven days a week. As her older brother and sister had already moved out, seven-year-old Mary was responsible for looking after her father, bedridden with tuberculosis. Mary would later credit her indomitable spirit to her mother, who always exhorted her with the words, "You can do it."

Although Mary was academically inclined, her parents

could not afford to send her to college, and instead, she married Ben Rogers, a radio personality in Houston who played with a local band, the Hawaiian Strummers. Unable to manage financially on their own, the young couple moved in with Mary's family, which grew to include her and Ben's three children.

During her marriage, Mary was often in the role of a single mother, as her husband was often financially and emotionally absent. To bring in an income, Mary worked at door-to-door sales jobs, relying on the commissions for much-needed revenue. In order to improve her chances at success, she managed to enroll in the University of Houston, with the goal of becoming a doctor. However, the dream of college came to an abrupt end during her first semester. Rogers, who had been drafted during World War II, returned home and filed for divorce. In the past year, he had been strumming more than his guitar.

Although the marriage had been shaky, Mary took the news hard and was bombarded with feelings of hurt, humiliation, and depression. This was compounded by the onslaught of symptoms of rheumatoid arthritis. She described this as "the lowest point of my life." However, remembering her mother's mantra, "You can do it," she managed to put herself together and resumed working in door-to-door sales. In order to earn a more stable income, she started working for Stanley Home Products in 1939.

Although petite, she lugged heavy household cleaning products and became the queen of sales. Proud of her accomplishments in the workforce, she was embittered by her company's policy of denying her a promotion up the corporate ladder because of her gender. In 1952, angered that she could never move to a higher position, she quit after twenty-five years.

Mary Kathlyn crossed her fingers and moved to Dallas to work for the company World Gift. There her sales record was so spectacular that in one year she single-handedly increased profits by 50 percent. Again she was plagued with health problems; she developed a tic that distorted her face. Although self-conscious about her appearance, she took to wearing oversized sunglasses until she could afford medical treatment, and kept up her frenetic work schedule. However, in her new position, her abilities and business acumen were once again glossed over because she was a woman in a suit-and-tie world.

After eleven years, the last straw was when she was passed over for promotion in favor of a man whom she had trained. Not only did he rise higher in the corporate hierarchy, but he also received twice her salary, despite having been employed for one year. She quit in disgust. Recalling her outrage, she said, "Those men didn't believe a woman had brain matter at all. I learned back then that, as long as men didn't believe women could do anything, women were never going to have a chance."

Mary Kathlyn found herself forty-five and unemployed. She did not feel that a woman's place was in the home. However, after two disillusioning forays into the business world, it was where she was situated. Determined to do something productive, she decided to write a how-to book for women, outlining the knowledge she had gained in her years as a very successful, albeit low-level salesperson. Its message would be to inspire women to take the reins in the male-dominated world of business, and to deliver the message that dreams were not just for sleeping.

To start off her book, which she worked on at her kitchen table, she devised a list of all the negative and positive things she had observed working for her previous employers. After staring at them, she slapped her hand to her platinum head, enthused by her eureka moment: She had committed to paper the perfect plan for a successful company. She was so confident of her vision that she abandoned her writing and decided to transform her idea into reality. She later recalled, "I began asking myself: Why are you theorizing about a dream company? Why don't you just start one?" The book would have to wait twenty years.

Now that she had the blueprint for her business venture, she needed a product. She purchased a skin-care formula from an Arkansas tanner named J. W. Heath, who had inadvertently stumbled on the cream when he noticed that his hands stayed soft and wrinkle-free (unlike his face) while he worked on his hides. She bought his invention for $500 from his daughter Ova Spoonemore, whom she'd met years earlier at a Stanley Home Products party. Ova would hand out the creams, explaining to the women that they were her guinea pigs. Mary Kathlyn invested the rest of her $5,000 life savings to launch her brainchild.

Around the same time she married George Hallenbeck, who was to be in charge of company finances. However, only one month before the business was to debut, he died of a heart attack. His widow persevered. She brought her twenty-year-old son, Richard Rogers, into her late husband's end of the business.

The company, Beauty by Mary Kay, opened on Friday, September 13, 1963. She set up shop in a five-hundred-square-foot Dallas storefront with nine of her girlfriends. She chose pink for her packaging. Out of the original tanner product she introduced five lotions, and borrowing from the "house party" model she had participated in during her days at Stanley, a Beauty representative would invite her friends over for a "free" facial and then pitch the products. Mary guided her female sales force with her philosophy that their priorities should be God first, family second, and career third.

One of the perks for the saleswomen was that they could work their own schedules, enabling them to juggle their dual roles of homemaker and working woman. What also made the company an enticing place to work was the staunch policy of equal pay for equal work, something corporate America was not offering its female workforce. Of this, Mary later said, "Instead of a door marked 'For Men Only,' our company opened its doors wide with welcome—especially for women." In an era when women could not sign their names on a bank loan, Mary Kay offered them financial opportunities as well as self-esteem.

The recipe that this feisty woman had cooked up at her kitchen table worked, even beyond her wildest dreams. By the year's end, Beauty cosmetics had racked up $198,000 in sales. In alchemist fashion, she had parlayed a hide tanner's cream and the color pink into gold. To celebrate, in 1964, the glitzy icon of free enterprise organized her first sales convention, which she termed a seminar. It was held in a warehouse covered with balloons and crepe paper. She cooked chicken and made Jell-O salad, which she served on paper plates to her two-hundred-strong sales force.

From the onset, the seminars were emotional affairs, where tears were as copious as the trademark pink of the packaging. There Mary would echo her mother's maxim of "You can do it" amid raucous applause. By her side was her third husband, Melville Jerome Ash.

One of the grand dame of marketing's most savvy strategies was offering her consultants (as she called her sales force) incentives, their "Cinderella gifts." The top sellers were rewarded with diamond bee pins and pink Cadillacs. The metaphor of the bee is explained in her quotation, "Aerodynamically the bumblebee shouldn't be able to fly, but the bumblebee doesn't know that so it goes on flying anyways."

Mary Kay Ash, the high priestess of pink, celebrated her success in her $5 million thirty-room pink palace—in its garage, her own pink Cadillac. Each summer she marshaled her troops from around the world to Dallas for an annual extravaganza that was equal parts sales convention, Las Vegas show, and old-time revival. In answer to the question of how she succeeded so quickly, she said, "The answer is I was middle-aged, had varicose veins, and I didn't have time to fool around. Have you heard the definition of a woman's needs? From fourteen to forty, she needs good looks, from forty to sixty, she needs personality, and I'm here to tell you that after sixty, she needs cash."

A friend once commented to the cosmetic queen that "Mary Kay Cosmetics was a divine accident looking for a place to happen." Perhaps the term "divine accident" is an apt way to describe her eureka, which resulted in a pink empire that shattered the male glass ceiling and allowed women everywhere to emulate Mary Kay's mantra: "*We* can do it."

- The Ashes' family fortune is estimated at $325 million.
- Mary Kay Cosmetics gives away pink Cadillacs in the United States, pink Toyotas in Taiwan, pink Fords in Argentina, pink Volvos in the Nordic countries, pink Volkswagens in China, and pink Mercedeses in Germany.
- In 1993, Mary Kay opened the Mary Kay Museum in Texas, where the flashy gowns she wore during her seminars are preserved on Mary Kay mannequins.
- PETA achieved a victory when Mary Kay Cosmetics put a moratorium on animal testing and giving away fur coats as incentives.

Eureka #31
(1963)

In a plane above New York City, a wife had a eureka moment that made her husband a household name and his bank account Midas' own. He accomplished this by turning her eureka into a concept whose name connotes grave danger yet paradoxically produced pure gold.

Buddy was born in California to a family hit by the Depression. He was a pudgy kid who preferred music over sports. When he dropped out of the University of San Francisco, it was to pursue his dream of becoming a professional entertainer, but his father dissuaded him, arguing that earning a living that way would be impractical. Following paternal advice, Buddy obtained a position as a bank clerk. However, the first day on the job, he discovered that the teller next to him had been there for almost three decades and was still only earning a pittance. He took that as a wake-up call and quit. Shortly afterward, he was drafted into World War II but was rejected because of his girth.

With the doors of banking and the military shutting in his face, Buddy once more turned to his first love, singing. At age nineteen, he obtained a job as a radio singer on *San Francisco Sketchbook*, where he earned $100 a week. On the show he was billed as "the young romantic voice of radio." He attracted the interest of an RKO studio boss, who set up a meeting; it didn't go well. He later recalled, "As soon as I walked into their hotel room, I could see their faces fall. Rather than the handsome crooner they had anticipated, they saw a very overweight man." Sensing their disappointment, he started the first of his lifelong diets and, armed with determination, lost eighty pounds in four months. His newfound confidence in his appearance led him from radio to the new medium of television.

From 1958 to 1962, he hosted a game show called *Play Your Hunch*, and when Jack Paar accidentally wandered onto the set during a live broadcast, Buddy interviewed him. This helped him launch his own talk show on NBC in 1962 under his birth name: *The Merv Griffin Show*. The show was syndicated in 1965 and stayed on the air in various incarnations until he retired in 1986.

Although very successful, the host often had conflicts with the network executives, especially in regard to his choice of controversial guests. They were not impressed when stripper Gypsy Rose Lee dropped her drawers or when Merv invited Christine Jorgensen, the first man to successfully undergo a sex-change operation, to the set. One of his greatest coups was when Dr. Martin Luther King Jr. gave him the only sit-down interview he ever granted. He recalls, "To see him sit down there—he makes the audience laugh, and you see a whole person instead of a podium and a million people in front of him at the Lincoln Memorial." Sometimes the king of the talk show was himself dethroned, as happened when he interviewed Al Pacino. When he asked the actor how he had made it from the Bronx to Broadway, Pacino answered, "By subway." Merv said the only one of his guests who ever intimidated him was Rose Kennedy. Griffin said what he discovered by interviewing hundreds of people is "that there's a major story behind everyone."

In 1964, Merv struggled with ideas for a new game show while flying back to New York. His wife, Julann, was concurring about how boring the current shows were. She attributed this to the fact that instead of using information, they depended on what she called "asinine showing off." It was in midair that Julann had her eureka moment: She suggested to Merv a quiz show in reverse, one where the host would provide the answers. Merv was at first taken aback: The show *Twenty One* had culminated in a Congressional investigation after the most telegenic contestants were given the answers. Merv assumed his wife was joking, but then she engaged Merv in a rapid-fire answer-and-question session.

Julann: The answer is 5,280.
Merv: How many feet are in a mile?
Julann: The answer is 52 Wistful Vista.
Merv: Where did Fibber McGee and Molly live?
Julann: The answer is Cathy Fiscus.
Merv: What is the name of the little girl that fell in the well in the 1930s?

By the time the Griffins landed in the Big Apple, they knew they had stumbled on a good idea. After further development, the Griffins pitched their brainchild, which they called *What's the Question?* During the presentation, Griffin explained there were to be six categories, wherein executive Ed Vane stated he felt the game needed "more jeopardies." The remark triggered a respondent chord. Contestants would be "in jeopardy" because incorrect responses would be penalized by a deduction in the player's overall score.

The show turned out to be a tough sell, but not for the reasons the couple had predicted. As Julann recalls, "NBC flipped for the idea, but they thought the questions were too hard. But then, they were network executives, so of course they would think it was too hard. So we made the questions easier until they said it was ready to air."

The Griffins made television history with the first episode of *Jeopardy!* Its first Final Jeopardy answer was in the category of Famous Quotes: "Good night, sweet prince." The correct answer: "Who is Hamlet?" The series earned a place of prominence in American pop culture and paved the way for dozens of game shows that followed on its knowledge-based heels. Because of its phenomenal success, Merv was able to build a television empire, Merv Griffin Enterprises, which went on to include another mega-hit, one in which a certain elegantly sheathed Vanna made letter turning into a seductive art: *The Wheel of Fortune.* The name could serve as a metaphor for Merv Griffin's life.

As with all wheels of fortune, Merv Griffin's also turned. In 1969, CBS offered Griffin a late-night show opposite Johnny Carson, but it failed a year later. The network disapproved of

Griffin's guests, many of whom spoke out against the Vietnam War. For example, CBS blurred the image of political activist Abbie Hoffman because he was satirically wearing his trademark American flag shirt. Griffin disliked being censored and complained, until he was fired by CBS.

In 1976, his marriage to Julann unraveled due to irreconcilable differences. His great wealth also contributed to two lawsuits from two men, who demanded hundreds of millions of dollars, providing tabloid fodder to a public hungry for the lowdown on the lofty. Perhaps it was to silence them that he began seeing Eva Gabor. One result of their relationship was that his prize horses all sported Gabor's shade of red lipstick. When questioned about his sexuality in a *New York Times* interview, Griffin camouflaged his heartache with a wisecrack: "I tell everybody that I'm quarter-sexual. I will do anything with anybody for a quarter."

Merv's wealth escalated to such an extent that in the late 1980s, the West and East Coast titans, Griffin and Donald Trump, were involved in a financial tug-of-war over the purchase of some Atlantic City hotel casinos. When Trump discovered who he was bidding against, he patronizingly inquired, "You mean that band singer?" The press came back to Merv with that tidbit and asked if he had a rejoinder. He replied, "No. Just tell him to behave himself or I'll go around to Atlantic City and take the T off his name."

In his eighties, the Hollywood heavyweight finally abandoned his lifelong diets. He explained, "I've outlived all my diet doctors. My first doctor was Dr. Atkins. And then I went through Dr. Stillman, the water diet. I think he drowned on his own diet. And I had Dr. Tarnover, and his girlfriend shot him. So I gave up dieting." In the last years of his life, he never lost his most faithful sidekick, his sense of humor. He told the *New York Times* that he was happy: "I've got great energy, and I've got all my hair."

A final question concerning Merv Griffin could have been the one from his first episode of *Jeopardy!* "Good night, sweet prince." Answer: "What would have been a fitting eulogy for Merv Griffin?"

- In 2001, *TV Guide* ranked *Jeopardy!* as #2 among the 50 Greatest Game Shows of all time; *Esquire* named it the magazine's favorite game show.
- In a week devoted to Washington "power players," Bob Woodward missed a question about *All the President's Men*.
- Griffin's tombstone, at his request, is engraved, "I will not be right back after this message."
- In its earliest days, *Jeopardy!* contestants would not be given credit unless their response was grammatically correct.
- Merv and Nancy Reagan exchanged birthday greetings every July 6, their shared birth date. Griffin was an honorary pallbearer at Ronald Reagan's funeral.

Eureka #32
(1964)

One of the unintended consequences of Napoleon's Egyptian campaign was the discovery of the 1,676-pound, circa 196 BC Rosetta stone. However, the archaeological treasure did not merely unlock the enigma of hieroglyphics, it also resulted in a eureka moment that led to a man and his people reconnecting with their roots.

Walt Whitman wrote, "The hand that rocks the cradle rules the world." However, in Henning, Tennessee, in the 1920s, it was Cynthia Palmer, sitting on her rocking chair on her front porch, who molded her grandson's life. She would recount stories from her own grandmother, words that had become her family's mythology. Alex Haley's mother voiced her disapproval of these conversations: "I wish you would quit talking about that old-timey slavery stuff; it's entirely embarrassing." She wanted her son to grow up with an eye to his future, not his past. However, Cynthia disregarded her daughter's request, feeling that where one came from was vital.

During World War II, at age eighteen, Alex enlisted in the Coast Guard as a kitchen mess boy, serving white officers. In order to stave off the boredom of long days on board a ship in the South Pacific, he first turned to reading words and then writing them. When his shipmates realized his command of language, they paid him to ghostwrite love letters to their wives and girlfriends. His portable typewriter became his most prized possession.

After twenty years of service, Alex traded the sea for a position at *Reader's Digest*, where he published articles on people who had lived notable lives; little did he realize that one day his own would qualify. He also freelanced for Hugh Hefner, and initiated what was to become a staple of the magazine: the *Playboy* interviews. They ran the gamut from American Nazi Party leader George Lincoln Rockwell, who only agreed to meet with Haley after a phone call in which he demanded assurance that Alex wasn't a Jew, to famous black celebrities. He interviewed Dr. Martin Luther King Jr. (which was the lengthiest interview the Civil Rights leader ever gave to a publication) and Cassius Clay (who explained why he was changing his name to Muhammad Ali). However, the interview that cast Haley into the literary limelight was the one that led to the classic *The Autobiography of Malcolm X as Told to Alex Haley*. Two weeks after the manuscript was completed, Malcolm X was assassinated, and Haley's work became the sole official record of his tumultuous life.

Following the publication of the book, *Reader's Digest* sent Haley to London for an assignment. While there, the avid student of history went to the British Museum, unaware that the visit was going to result in his life's metamorphosis. There he became transfixed by a tablet, the Rosetta stone; its decipherment proved the key that unlocked more than five thousand years of human history. The Rosetta stone led to his eureka moment: Just as the artifact had revealed the meaning of hieroglyphics, his grandmother's stories, told to the accompaniment of the rhythmic rocking, could whisper the secrets of his family's African past. He realized he should write a book on his family's genealogy that would, in turn, be a microcosm of the larger black American experience. He purchased a book on the archaeological marvel and resolved to embark on a quest to crack the code of his history. The artifact had become the compass that would determine the course of his life's mission.

Fired with enthusiasm, he contacted Lila Acheson Wallace, who agreed to finance his research because it would make for a groundbreaking article in her magazine, *Reader's Digest*. For the next year, Haley was a constant fixture in the National Archives in Washington, DC, where he pored over post–Civil War records. He also traced the route his ancestors had traveled as slaves living in the South. His gut-wrenching moment arrived when he stumbled on the 1800 census with the names of his maternal great-grandparents. Based on this information and the stories that had fired his imagination as a child, he embarked on a twelve-year odyssey. He traveled by safari to his ancestral Mandingo village, where he met with a griot—an oral historian—who told him about his forefather, Kunta Kinte, who had been abducted from the small village of Juffure in the Gambia, West Africa, on the slave ship *Ligonier*. From his research, Haley knew that Kunta Kinte had arrived in Maryland in 1767 and had been sold to a plantation owner in Virginia. The skeletal story of *Roots* had taken shape. His next step was to give it flesh.

Because his high-rise apartment was not conducive to penning his epic, Haley booked his return passage to the United States on a freight ship, the *African Star*, so that he could simulate the slaves' three-month crossing. For even further verisimilitude, he removed his clothes and lay down in the dark, freezing quarters in the bottom of the ship. There he tried his utmost to imagine Kunta Kinte's terror. He attempted to conceptualize what it was like to be ripped from one's home, shackled amid human waste, dreading an unknown fate. Haley listened to the night and heard voices: his grandmother's, Chicken George's, Kizzy's, and Kunta's.

In 1976, the 688-page book *Roots: The Saga of an American Family* unleashed a storm of interest in genealogy and an empathy for the black experience. It became the number one national bestseller, and to date 6 million copies have been sold. Alex Haley had become the American griot. Further acclaim followed when *Roots* became a six-night television miniseries, with a record-breaking audience of 130 million viewers. The audience surpassed that of *Gone With the Wind*; its finale is the third highest rated U.S. program, only exceeded by the last episode of *M*A*S*H** and Super Bowl XLII.

Alex Haley had traveled far from Coast Guard mess boy; he had gained honor, wealth, and fame. Despite winning the National Book Award and the Pulitzer Prize, Haley claimed that the most emotional moment of his life was when he stood on the site in Annapolis, Maryland, where his ancestor had arrived in shackles two hundred years before.

However, all of his accomplishments were not enough to

shield him from fate's slings and arrows. After his third divorce, he declared, "I'm just not a stationary husband." He was also accused of plagiarizing another book in parts of *Roots*, and the judge declared, "Copying there is, period." Haley agreed to an out-of-court settlement of $650,000.

When Alex Haley passed away in 1992, posthumous honors were given to the South's famous son. A memorial to Alex Haley and Kunta Kinte was unveiled to commemorate the historic location where Haley's ancestor had arrived. His childhood front porch, whose landscape had influenced his destiny, was made into a state historical monument, and his body was interred in front of it. His home became the first museum devoted entirely to a black Tennessean. Its walls showcase numerous photographs and memorabilia from his life, though the greatest source of biographical information lies in the pages of *Roots*. It was an epic born from a eureka moment, inspired by words spoken from a rocking chair in Henning, Tennessee, and letters written on an ancient Egyptian stone.

- Haley served as a ghostwriter for John F. Kennedy's *Profiles in Courage*, although his contribution was of a stylized, editing nature.
- In 2006, Ilyasah Shabazz, the daughter of Malcolm X, encouraging the reading of Haley's books.
- Alex Haley narrated the last few minutes of the miniseries *Roots*.

Eureka #33
(1965)

The word "holiday" derives from "holy" and "day," and most religions trace their holidays to ancient, spiritual events, ones that molded the course of world history. However, one holiday had a far different birth: It was conceived in the modern era rather than in biblical times, and its inspiration stemmed not from an act of love but from an act of hate.

Ronald Everett was born on a poultry farm in Maryland, the fourteenth child of a Baptist minister. In the late 1950s, he moved to California to attend Los Angeles City College, where he became the first African American president of the student body. He later attended UCLA, where he received a master's degree in political science and African studies. A major impact on his life was a 1960 meeting with Malcolm X, who espoused the view that blacks must return to Africa culturally and spiritually, even if not physically. Similarly, just as Malcolm X had repudiated his birth surname of Little because he felt it was a mark of shame from his ancestors' slave owners, Everett adopted the title of Maulana, Swahili for "master teacher," and Africanized Everett to Karenga, Swahili for "nationalist."

In 1965, Karenga created a UCLA campus group called US, an acronym for United Slaves. He also christened it with that title because of its implicit reference to "them." He said of its inception that it was founded as the sons and daughters of Malcolm X, and as an heir to his legacy. All members of US were required to adopt African surnames, learn Swahili, shave their heads, and wear traditional tribal garb. Karenga, in his book *The Quotable Karenga*, exhorted US to follow the seven principles of blackness: "Think black, talk black, act black, create black, buy black, vote black, and live black."

Karenga had been heavily enmeshed in black nationalism for a few years when, in 1965, a white police officer arrested a black motorist on charges of intoxication. The incident created a spark that ignited the simmering racial tension in the Watts neighborhood of Los Angeles. The violence escalated to such a degree that martial law was declared and the National Guard was called in to restore order. When it ended, thirty-four people had been killed and over a thousand were injured. Karenga was distraught at the loss of life. He was also upset with the images of looting and mayhem that white America associated with his black brothers.

Two days after the race riot, Dr. King gave an impassioned speech pleading for peace. Karenga then wondered what he could do. He felt what was needed was a galvanizing force that would restore a sense of pride in his people's heritage while providing solidarity among the residents of Watts, as well as African Americans around the country.

This led to Karenga's eureka moment: He would create a holiday to celebrate black culture. Participants would wear traditional African attire, and it would center around seven humanist principles. Each night a candle would be lit in deference to each of its ideals. He chose the Swahili word *Kwanzaa*, which is a translation of "first fruits," a reference to an ancient African tradition. He determined that it should be a weeklong observance to coincide with the traditional mainstream holidays from which he felt alienated. Instead of "Merry Christmas" or "Happy Chanukah," its greeting would be "Habari Gani?" which translates to "What's the news?"

On December 26, 1966, Ron Karenga and his family and friends lit the unity candle, and the tradition of Kwanzaa was officially born. From the horrors of the Watts riot came a holiday that brought families and communities together to support each other in an affirmative way, to reflect on the past year's blessings, and to find pride in their unique ancestral heritage.

Unfortunately, in 1969, the answer to the greeting "Habari Gani?" was extremely negative. In that year, the US organization clashed with the Black Panthers over who should head the new Afro-American Studies Center at UCLA, and both groups started bringing guns to campus. An altercation ensued, which resulted in the murder of two members of the Black Panthers. More horrific news was to follow.

In 1971, Karenga became paranoid that the FBI had infiltrated US and believed that two female members were trying to kill him. The women claimed that for two days they were held hostage, during which they were stripped and whipped, and had detergent and running hoses placed in their mouths. Karenga was arrested and sentenced to up to ten years in California State Prison.

In jail, Karenga once more emulated his role model, Malcolm X. He studied voraciously and earned a doctorate. However, unlike Malcolm, Karenga turned to Marxism rather than Islam. He believed that egalitarianism would unite his people. Four years later, when he was released, the angry young man had disappeared, and a leader had emerged. In 1979, he was hired as head of the Black Studies Department at California State University in Long Beach, a post that he held until 2002.

In his role as a respected spokesperson, he argued for reason to prevail after the 1992 riots in Los Angeles, following the police beating of Rodney King. While the trial was under way, Dr. Karenga told *Newsweek*, "L.A. can be a model in a positive way or a negative way."

The Kwanzaa holiday remains Karenga's most important legacy. In the 1990s, his brainchild was celebrated by more than 18 million people in the United States, Canada, the Caribbean, Europe, and Africa. A hallmark of its national legitimacy was displayed in 2004 when the U.S. Postal Service issued a stamp in honor of Kwanzaa; it depicts seven figures in colorful robes symbolizing the seven principles. Karenga and his wife, Tiamoya, have presided over hundreds of celebrations all over the world, in manifestations of family love and black unity. In view of the historic inauguration of America's first African American president, the Kwanzaa greeting of "Habari Gani?" can, at last, be answered in the affirmative.

- In 1995, Karenga authored the mission statement of the Million Man March.
- *The Black Candle*, a documentary narrated by Maya Angelou, is a 2008 film about the holiday.

Eureka #34
(1966)

Occasionally from acts of great horror arise acts of great honor. This was the case in the saga of two sisters, one tragic, the other triumphant, who were responsible for lighting a torch whose flames have illuminated the lives of millions.

Blessed with great wealth and prestige, Joseph Kennedy demanded greatness from his nine offspring. His message to his children was, "The important thing is win—don't come in second or third, that doesn't count—but win, win, win." His daughter, Eunice, did not disappoint.

Rather than resting on a debutante's laurels, she received a degree in sociology from Stanford in 1943. Postgraduation, she embarked on a career devoted to public service: She headed a juvenile delinquency project through the Department of Justice, and then became a social worker at the Penitentiary for Women in Virginia. Her social activism stemmed from her parents' recitation of the biblical injunction, "Much is expected of those to whom much has been given."

In 1953, in St. Patrick's Cathedral in New York City, she married Robert Sargent Shriver, a match to whom her family gave an enthusiastic thumbs-up. Sargent, a graduate of Yale Law School, would later serve as the U.S. ambassador to France and run as the Democratic vice presidential candidate in 1972. His list of accomplishments would one day include first director of the Peace Corps and part owner of the Baltimore Orioles. The couple shared the commonality of devout Catholicism; his well-worn rosary went wherever he did.

Eunice and Sargent had five children, who were raised to share their parents' strong sense of social conscience. Despite the demands of marriage to a high-profile husband and a large family, in 1957, Eunice took over the Joseph P. Kennedy Jr. Foundation, which had been established in the memory of her eldest brother, who had been killed in World War II. The foundation's goal was to help society in its acceptance of citizens afflicted with mental retardation.

Eunice traveled across the country, visiting the notorious facilities that were warehouses for retarded Americans. What she discovered were remote institutions where the mentally handicapped had been deposited into bleak, overcrowded wards. There they were relegated to "out-of-sight, out-of-mind," no longer members of society. Of these asylums she stated, "There was a complete lack of interest in the mentally retarded and lack of knowledge about their capabilities. They were isolated because their families were embarrassed and the public was prejudiced." In 1961, she tirelessly campaigned in her brother John's bid for the presidency. When he was elected, she had a pulpit from which to preach her advocacy for the mentally challenged. She was in the Oval Office when

John, at her behest, signed a bill she had championed to form the first President's Committee on Mental Retardation. Afterward, he handed his sister his pen as a keepsake.

However, her interest in helping the mentally challenged changed from professional to personal because of a phone call. A distraught mother contacted her with the heart-wrenching account of how her son had to spend his summers alone because no camp would accept a child with mental retardation. While other society women may have resolved the problem by writing a sizable donation, thereby discharging her noblesse oblige, Eunice took another course. Perhaps inspired by memories of her own childhood, during which she played quarterback against her brothers Jack and Ted in family games, she told the distraught mother, "You don't have to talk about it anymore. You come here a month from today. I'll start my own camp."

The camp she started was on the grounds of her home in Timberlawn, Maryland, a huge Civil War–era mansion with more than two hundred acres of grounds. With the support of her husband, who was initially skeptical, she enlisted nearly one hundred volunteers and set up activities, including floor hockey, baseball, soccer, volleyball, gymnastics, aquatics, and horseback riding. Soon a typical day at Camp Timberlawn would have scores of campers, counselors, horses, and obstacle courses spread over the compound. For five weeks every summer, fifty special athletes could have the time of their lives. When her daughter, Maria, married Arnold Schwarzenegger, Eunice drafted him as a coach. The attendees accomplished activities no one had believed they were capable of. Word spread, and soon similar camps sprung up across the United States and Canada. The doctors and experts had been proven wrong. Eunice Shriver would later say, "They're not accepted in the schools. They're not accepted in play programs. They're just not accepted. We have much to do."

In 1966, a physical education teacher named Anne McGlone Burke, who worked for the Chicago Park District, proposed holding a citywide track meet to raise awareness for the handicapped. She approached the Kennedy Foundation with her idea, and it was one that led to Eunice's eureka moment: She decided to create a Special Olympics.

On July 20, 1968, the first of the games was held in Chicago's Soldier Field, with a thousand athletes from the United States and Canada competing in athletics, floor hockey, and aquatics. In the opening ceremonies address, Shriver said, "The Chicago Special Olympics prove a very fundamental fact, the fact that exceptional children—children with mental retardation—can be exceptional athletes, the fact that through sports they can realize their potential for growth." Shriver, remembering her father's emphasis on winning as the only option, modified the definition of winning. At the opening game, she explained, "In ancient Rome, the gladiators went into the arena with these words on their lips: 'Let me win. But if I cannot win, let me be brave in the attempt. Let us begin the Olympics.'" However, merely by competing, all of the athletes were winners. No longer would differently gifted individuals and their families be sidelined; their own Olympic torch had been lit.

The inspiration for the project was Rosemary Kennedy. She was the eldest daughter, Eunice's older sister, and was institutionalized for most of her life. In a family of overachievers, her intellectual limitations loomed large. Her shortcomings were a source of consternation to the patrician patriarch Joseph. When Rosemary was sixteen, she wrote to him, "I would do anything to make you so happy. I hate to disappoint you in any way."

In her teen years, she became increasingly difficult. This was probably due to typical adolescent hormones as well as her feelings of insecurity, fueled by her father's attitude toward her. She was sent to a convent; however, she was often discovered sneaking out at night. Joseph, who had his eyes on the prize of the presidency for his son, was extremely anxious that Rosemary not create a family scandal. He worried the Kennedys' Roman Catholicism would be enough of a political impediment without adding another. John F. Kennedy later stated, "I am not the Catholic candidate for president. I am the Democratic Party's candidate for president, who happens also to be a Catholic."

In 1941, when Rosemary was twenty-three, doctors told Joseph they could perform an operation that would control her outbursts. The surgeon who performed the lobotomy, Dr. James Watts, later explained the procedure by saying they made an incision in her brain. As he cut, a fellow surgeon, Dr. Walter Freeman, kept Rosemary talking by having her recite the Lord's Prayer and "God Bless America" and counting backward. He said, "We made an estimate on how far to cut based on how she responded. When she began to become incoherent, we stopped." The lobotomy stopped Rosemary's outbursts; however, it also left her incontinent, and her conversational skills were reduced to an unintelligible babble. Rose Kennedy, who had not been told of the operation, was furious that her daughter's life had been stolen from her. This incident fueled her anger against her husband even more than his ongoing affair with Gloria Swanson.

Rosemary was eventually sent to Wisconsin, to the St. Coletta School for Exceptional Children, which had formerly been known as St. Coletta's Institute for Backward Children. She became the forgotten Kennedy, but not by Eunice, who continued to visit her beloved sister, whom she called Rosie. She was the inspiration who launched Eunice on the path of helping bring the mentally disabled into mainstream society and thereby transforming them from institutionalized outcasts to family members, neighbors, and athletes. Loretta Claiborne, a Special Olympian, said of Eunice, who was her mentor, "I think she teaches that no matter who you are, you are no different than the next person. To me, I think she's hope."

Eunice Kennedy Shriver passed away in 2009, surrounded by her husband, five children, and nineteen grandchildren. However, because of her life of service, her death was not just her family's loss but America's. President Barack Obama said Shriver will be remembered "as a champion for people with intellectual disabilities and as an extraordinary woman who, as much as anyone, taught our nation—and our world—that no physical or mental barrier can restrain the power of the human spirit."

Eunice Shriver's inspired idea to institute the Special Olympics ignited a torch that shines on special athletes, which, in turn, shines on us all. Through her brainchild, she stepped out of the long shadow cast by brothers John, Robert, and Edward, and fulfilled her parents' injunction, "Much is expected of those to whom much has been given."

- John F. Kennedy was so interested in Eunice's research on the mentally challenged that he broke away from one of the emergency meetings on the Cuban Missile Crisis on October 15, 1962, to receive her report.

- Anthony Shriver, the youngest of Eunice's five children, organized a group called Best Buddies, in which college students and other individuals are paired in one-on-one friendships with mentally challenged people. It has 6,500 members.

- The Special Olympics has united warring factions: In 1993, in South Africa, white and black athletes competed together for the first time; in 1994, Jews and Arabs participated together; in 2005, in Afghanistan, women competed alongside men.

Eureka #35
(1971)

London in the dawn of the 1970s was a hotbed of the burgeoning counterculture, whose anthem was rock 'n' roll. British musicians acted as Pied Pipers to thousands of devotees, who were drawn to their idols' drumbeat. Two Americans were part of this movement, and it was their shared eureka moment, born from the longing for the comfort foods of home, that left an imprint on the world of rock.

It was against this backdrop that the quintessential odd couple met. Isaac Tigrett was a native of Tennessee, who had moved, at age fifteen, with his affluent family to England, where his father exported vintage Rolls-Royces to the United States. After attending private school in Switzerland, he traveled the hippie trail to India on a spiritual quest before returning to London. There he traded his Southern Baptist religion for Eastern mysticism.

Peter Morton, the scion of a restaurant family best known for Morton's Steakhouse of Chicago, had arrived in England in

1969 after earning his business degree from the University of Denver. His trip abroad was a postgraduate stint before embarking in a position with a Wall Street conglomerate. When Isaac and Peter ran into each other, they found themselves wishing they could forgo British fish and chips for American burgers and fries. Their longing led to a eureka moment: There were thousands of American expatriates, appetites watering for the same food. They decided to do something about the perceived cuisine gap.

Tigrett and Morton, although they were possessors of very divergent personalities, agreed on their vision for their restaurant. Its menu would offer American staples of burgers, fries, shakes, apple pie, and cold beer. Unlike its neighboring elitist establishments, where dress codes and propriety were strictly enforced, all would be welcome, and prices would not reflect blue-blood status. This egalitarian philosophy was reflected in its motto, which Tigrett had seen at an Indian café: "Love All—Serve All." To make their restaurant even more unique, they decided on a theme of rock—a novel concept, as there were no other themed restaurants at the time.

With money borrowed from their parents, they only needed to christen their establishment, which had been converted from a Rolls-Royce showroom. Tigrett came up with the name after looking at the back of the Doors' 1970 album, *Morrison Hotel.* On it was a picture of a make-believe cocktail bar called the Hard Rock Café—and on June 14, 1971, it opened its doors.

The quirky restaurant, founded with low-key expectations (they were anxious that it would turn into the hard-knocks café), surpassed its owners' wildest dreams. Almost immediately queues snaked halfway down Piccadilly and rivaled those at Madame Tussauds. Celebrities began patronizing the music/food emporium, and their fame and antics served to further enhance the restaurant's rapidly growing reputation. The Beatles were some of the initial visitors, and Paul McCartney, Prince, Janet Jackson, Sting, Elton John, and George Harrison ended up performing. The Rolling Stones also added to the raucous ambience, and Led Zeppelin sent whiskey bottles crashing against the walls. Carole King immortalized the café when she wrote a tribute song to it. However, serendipity was soon to step in, which was to provide the American brainchild with its signature trademark.

Eric Clapton, the original guitar god and café regular, asked Tigrett if he would put up a plaque to reserve his favorite table. When the owner replied that his restaurant didn't do plaques, Eric asked if he would put up his guitar instead. Tigrett agreed. A short time later, Clapton sent over his red Fender Lead II, and it was placed over the coveted table. When Pete Townshend spied it, he sent over his Gibson Les Paul with a note, "Mine's as good as his! Love, Pete." This was the genesis of the décor of rock memorabilia that became the restaurant's most viable asset. The walls were soon showcasing outfits from world tours and rare photographs of legendary performers.

The café, in addition to its food, music, and stars, soon became a Smithsonian of rock 'n' roll; among its 70,000 objects: Madonna's first pointed bustier, a coat bearing Elvis Presley's initials, the Beatles' five-ton Magical Mystery Tour bus, and John Lennon's handwritten "Imagine." Its notoriety soon lured in celebrities even outside the world of rock: The Duke of

Westminster stopped by, and Steven Spielberg ate lunch there every day during the filming of *Raiders of the Lost Ark*.

Tigrett and Morton, the John and Paul of their rock crown jewel, perceiving that their lark had morphed into a landmark, decided to expand their London establishment, and it became a global conglomerate. However, along the way, the relationship between the two founders became contentious. The strain intensified when Tigrett became a Hindu convert and devoted follower of Indian guru Sai Baba. He moved in with Ringo Starr's ex-wife, Maureen Starkey, whom he later married. He lovingly referred to her as "his most authentic rock 'n' roll memorabilia." By the end of the 1970s, Tigrett's doctrine of "love all" no longer included Morton. Tigrett remained at heart a hippie activist, with his emblematic long hair and, in tribute to his Tennessee heritage, snakeskin boots. In contrast, Morton remained at heart the son of a scion, sporting Savile Row–tailored blue blazers and designer shoes. Not surprisingly, they moved in different circles: Tigrett's involved hippies, artists, and musicians, while Morton's involved models and fashion designers.

In 1988, Tigrett sold his interests in the Hard Rock Café for $108 million and headed to India for an ashram existence. However, his guru had other plans. Tigrett recalls, "My master said, 'I want you in the world—but not *of the* world.'" Sai Baba's mandate and Tigrett's own passion for music inspired him to open up the House of Blues in 1992 with his friend Dan Aykroyd.

Currently, Tigrett lives in a spacious Mediterranean-style home, overflowing with sacred objects from the East as well as fifteenth- and sixteenth-century Italian religious paintings.

He dresses entirely in black, right down to his cowboy boots. Isaac Tigrett's ongoing quest for spirituality has taken him on many paths. It is unknown what his next path will be; however, what is known *is* that it will involve music, and if precedent indicates the future, it will be successful.

Morton held on to his rock crown jewels for a few more years, until he sold them for $410 million. Hungry for his next venture, he opened up the desert playground of the rich and famous: the Hard Rock Hotel and Casino in Las Vegas. It was his vision to change the Strip from schlock to übercool. In his establishment there was nary a trace of a Liberace look-alike or an Elvis impersonator; however, one can spot Elton John's rhinestone piano. The crap tables are shaped like pianos, the one-armed bandits are shaped like Fender guitars, the chandeliers are made from gold-plated saxophones, and Harley-Davidsons are perched on top of the slot machines. The pièce de résistance is the hotel's pool, which occupies an expanse of land valued at $50 million. Morton sold it in 2006 for $770 million.

The rock mogul's current venture is his Los Angeles eatery, which bears his name; for almost twenty years, clout has been defined in Hollywood as the ability to get a table at his establishment. It is the venue for the powerhouse *Vanity Fair* party that takes place after the Oscars.

Little did the two young men in 1970s hippie-era London imagine their eureka moment would arrive through their mantra, "In rock we trust."

- The Seminole Tribe of Florida purchased the Hard Rock Café operation in 2006 for $965 million.

- There are 143 Hard Rock Cafés in over 36 countries.
- The largest Hard Rock Café is located in Orlando, Florida, and the second largest one is in Rio de Janeiro, Brazil.
- Tigrett's New York Hard Rock Café included the first guitar-shaped bar as well as a "God wall"—a tribute to the inspirational forces that guide people's lives. It featured a photograph of Sai Baba and an enormous Quaalude.

Eureka #36
(1980)

Sometimes a person finds a cause that becomes their grand passion, why Susan B. Anthony chained herself to a lamppost and why Mohandas Gandhi went on hunger fasts. One activist who found her calling was born in Britain, was raised in India, and discovered her eureka in America. Her mission was to give a voice to the voiceless.

Ingrid Ward was born in England, where her companions were a menagerie of pets. At age seven, the family moved to New Delhi, where Ingrid and her mother, alongside Mother Teresa, toiled in leper colonies. Mrs. Ward's philosophy was, "It doesn't matter who suffers, but how." One memory imprinted on Ingrid's mind occurred when a group of people had bound a dog's feet and had lowered him into a muddy ditch. Ingrid told members of the Ward's staff to bring in the tortured animal, who died in her arms.

At age eighteen, the family moved to Florida, where Ingrid met her husband, Steve Newkirk, a race-car driver. He introduced her to Formula One racing, in which, along with sumo wrestling, she developed a lifelong interest. She told the *New Yorker* about these hobbies, "It's sex. The first time you hear them rev their engines, my God! That noise goes straight up my spine!"

Ingrid and Steve moved to Maryland, where she studied to become a stockbroker. When a neighbor abandoned nineteen kittens, Ingrid took them to an animal shelter. A woman took them with the words, "Come in the back, and we will just put them down there." Ingrid misinterpreted the euphemism. When she heard that they had all been killed, she began to work at the shelter in order to alleviate the suffering of the animals.

Because the conditions were so horrific, she took to killing the animals herself, as the more humane alternative. She said of this experience, "And I just felt, to my bones, this cannot be right." Ingrid ended up blowing the whistle on the shelter and became an animal protection officer for the District of Columbia. She became DC's first female pound master and was named "Washingtonian of the Year." It was at this time, after a cruelty investigation at a farm, that she decided never again to eat anything that once had a face. She told a reporter, "I loved meat, liver above all." Her mantra became, "My test is if it screams and runs away when you go after it, don't eat it." However, this was only one of the many sacrifices she would make in her crusade for animal rights.

In 1980, Ingrid met the man, and the book, that were to alter the course of her life: fellow animal advocate Alex Pacheco. Alex had attended a Catholic university in Ohio, intending to become a priest. However, this plan was derailed when he visited a friend who worked in a meatpacking plant.

He was shocked when he witnessed two men throwing a newborn calf, cut from the uterus of its slaughtered mother, into a Dumpster. Later that week, he received a copy of a book by Australian Peter Sanger called *Animal Liberation*; he returned to Ohio a vegetarian. He changed his vocation from becoming a priest to devoting himself to what he called "other-than-human beings." For his efforts on behalf of livestock, he received anonymous death threats from farmers, who told him he was going to get his head blown off.

When Alex met Ingrid, he gave her *Animal Liberation*, which opposed "speciesism" and advocated that animals deserved equal moral consideration and rights. The book was a revelation to Ingrid. She said that before reading it, "I simply thought that people shouldn't cause animals unnecessary pain. I had never thought that maybe they don't belong to us, that they have their own place on the planet." The book led to Ingrid's eureka moment: to create PETA—People for the Ethical Treatment of Animals. *Animal Liberation* was to become the bible of the organization, which she would found based on its precepts.

Ingrid gave up on her career as a stockbroker to work full-time on behalf of animal rights. This decision, however, did not just impact those with fur and feathers. Steve Newkirk had married a woman who loved race-car driving, liver, and him, but now found himself married to an animal activist and vegetarian, who put the four-footed before her two-footed spouse. She was jailed twenty times for acts of civil disobedience, and the couple regularly received dead animals in their mailbox from the legions of whom Ingrid had enraged, putting further strain on the marriage. The couple divorced in

1980. The Newkirks had no children, as Ingrid had undergone sterilization at age twenty-two because she "came to think there was something wrong with wanting your own child" when there were so many orphans in the world.

Alex and Ingrid began living together, though they were as different as Jack Sprat and his wife: Ingrid was older, practical, and very organized, while Alex was absentminded and cared little about his personal appearance, dressing in painter's overalls and eating vegetarian hot dogs straight from the can. However, their dissimilarities paled in light of their great commonality: commitment to animal rights—a concept that was foreign in the 1980s.

At its onset, PETA consisted of what Newkirk later called "five people in a basement." Its tenets were drawn up at her kitchen table. Soon an event was to take place that would transform PETA into an international movement—one with 300 employees, 1.6 million members, and a $25 million annual budget.

In 1981, Alex, then a student at George Washington University, volunteered at the Institute of Behavioral Research in Silver Spring, Maryland, because he suspected animal abuse. Dr. Edward Taub, a psychologist, was experimenting on seventeen monkeys. He had cut their spinal cords and then used physical restraint, electric shock, and the withholding of food to force them to use their limbs. Although this was ostensibly done to further medical research, the method was barbaric, and the living conditions of the animals were appalling. Pacheco snuck into the lab at night to take photos, while Newkirk crouched in the backseat of a parked car outside, armed with a walkie-talkie to alert Alex if anyone entered the building. Their sting led to a police raid, which resulted in Dr. Taub being charged with 119 counts of animal cruelty. This was the first police raid on an animal research facility in the United States, and the first conviction of an animal researcher.

Newkirk and Pacheco were thrust into the public eye in the midst of their heady victory. Their action led to an amendment of the Animal Welfare Act in 1985, and it became the first animal rights case to be heard in front of the Supreme Court. PETA became a force to be reckoned with, and Newkirk became its fiery president. The mission statement of the fledging movement was "Animals are not ours to eat, wear, experiment on, or use for entertainment."

Because of the infamy surrounding the Silver Spring case, Newkirk became, to use Alex's words, a "press slut." She believes her grand gestures of civil disobedience are the best way to cut through what she cites as her greatest enemy, "human obliviousness." Because the case of the Silver Spring monkeys thrust Alex's picture into the limelight, it made it difficult for him to work undercover again. However, he continued to be active in other ways, which led to his undergoing forty arrests.

Ingrid arranged for PETA activists to throw a dead raccoon onto the table of Anna Wintour, the fur-supporting editor of *Vogue*, while she was dining at the Four Seasons Hotel in New York City, and leave bloody paw prints and the words "Fur Hag" on the steps of her home. A PETA member, who identified herself as Freda Fox, delivered a package of maggot-infested innards to Wintour's office in April 2000, explaining in a subsequent newspaper release, "Anna stole this animal's

skin and his life; she might as well have his guts." Wintour and
Vogue publisher Ron Galotti once retaliated against a PETA
protest outside the Condé Nast offices during the company's
annual Christmas party by sending down a plate of roast beef.
Two years later, PETA proved its bite was as sharp as its bark
during a Victoria's Secret lingerie show that was broadcast to
11 million viewers. Evading tight security, several women
managed to leap onto the stage in front of Brazilian supermodel Gisele Bündchen (dressed in a beaded bra and black
panties) with signs that read "Gisele: Fur Scum." This was in
reference to the *Blackglama* magazine ad that had featured
her wearing a black mink with the caption: "What becomes a
legend most?" The PETA women were immediately arrested,
amid a storm of publicity.

Another tactic was PETA's billboard campaign featuring
nude female celebrities with the slogan: "I'd rather go naked
than wear fur." Such practices have aroused the utmost ire, as
well as the utmost respect, for Ingrid Newkirk. However, the
president of PETA cares little for the world's approbation; all
she cares about is being "the voice for the voiceless."

The combination of a book by an Australian writer, the in-
vestigative work of an American student, and the crusading
spirit of a British activist united to make the world a more
humane place for nonhumans, giving voice to the voiceless.
And, in the end, that is what becomes a legend most.

- Newkirk's book, *Making Kind Choices*, has a foreword by Sir
  Paul McCartney. His daughter, Stella McCartney, is one of
  Ingrid's staunchest supporters and is the only major fashion
  designer to reject both fur and leather.

- In 2003, Newkirk publicized her will to draw attention to many of the practices she finds abhorrent. Newkirk has stated in her will that her skin be turned into wallets, her feet into umbrella stands (as elephant feet are used in India), and her flesh into "Newkirk Nuggets, and then grilled on a barbeque."

- PETA convinced cosmetics companies Avon, Estée Lauder, Revlon, and Mary Kay to stop testing their products on animals.

- In May 2006, two women held a naked protest near St. Paul's Cathedral in London to highlight the use of real bear fur in the bearskins used by the foot guards.

Eureka #37
(1982)

The Old Testament's most heartwarming example of female solidarity is the one that illustrates the love between Naomi and Ruth. A modern-day eureka stands as a testimony that the bond between two sisters is as powerful as the biblical one.

Susan and Nancy Goodman were raised in an affluent enclave in Peoria, Illinois. Their mother gave them a sacred task: "Fix what is wrong with the world." It was a message they took to heart. When they discovered that their friend was stricken with polio, the sisters hosted a song-and-dance revue as a fund-raiser, which raised $64. As the older sibling, Susan was always teaching Nancy the ropes.

As adults, Susan stayed in her hometown, where she married, had two children, and worked part-time as a model. Nancy, fond of horses and Texan culture, moved to Dallas, where she worked at Neiman Marcus, in the couture department, under the tutelage of Stanley Marcus. She married one of the store's executives, Robert Leitstein, and had her only child, Eric. To help bridge their distance, the sisters kept a 5 p.m. phone date. It was during one of these calls that Nancy heard shattering news: Susan had a lump in her breast.

During her sister's three-year battle against breast cancer, Nancy made dozens of trips to Peoria, despite having her own struggle: She was embroiled in a divorce. During their visits, Nancy was awed at how Susan coped with her hair loss and remained optimistic. Although Nancy did not realize it at the time, her big sister was still teaching her. Three years later, sitting in a hospital room, the thirty-six-year-old Susan asked her sister, on her deathbed, "to fix something that was wrong" in order to save other women from her fate: an agonizing death from breast cancer. Nancy promised that she would, even if the fight would consume the rest of her life. Believing herself unequal to fulfilling Susan's plea, Nancy tried to drown out a persistent, nagging question: "Could one person really make a difference?"

In 1980, while attending a fund-raiser, Nancy met Norman Brinker, the twice-married founder of the Bennigan's and Chili's restaurant chains, who was a father of five. He was empathetic to the loss of Nancy's sister; his first wife, tennis star Maureen Connolly, had died from ovarian cancer. The two married on Valentine's Day 1981.

The new Mrs. Brinker could have settled into a niche as the Texan wife of a multimillionaire—but she had a promise to keep. She desperately wanted to honor Susan's dying request, but she did not know how. She said, "My sister was my best friend, and when someone you love so much is looking at you, when they're dying, and asks you to do something that makes their life mean something, it's hard to say no." Nancy was also driven to help others because of the Judaic *Tikkun olam*, "fixing what is wrong with the world," taught by her mother.

Nancy decided the first step in eradicating her sister's killer was to get people talking about it. In that era, breast cancer was the disease that dare not speak its name. In Brinker's book, *The Race Is Won One Step at a Time*, she wrote, "I've always had the feeling that women's breasts were an easy topic of contemplation for men among themselves or in the bedroom, but discussing them with women in a dignified manner was a different story altogether."

Brinker's crusade became to bring breast cancer out of the bedroom closet. Nancy said at that time Americans were enraged at the loss of 58,000 soldiers killed in the Vietnam War, but no one was mentioning the death of 338,000 victims of breast cancer. Armed with $200 of her own money, a typewriter, and names jumbled together in a shoebox, she invited twenty friends to her home, and the Susan G. Komen Foundation was born. Though her husband had told her not to pester his wealthy friends, she had contacted every one of them by the next morning. In 1982, the oil business was booming in Texas, and donations amounting to a million dollars poured in. However, Nancy was not satisfied; Susan would have wanted more, deserved more.

The foundation was well on its way when life dealt Nancy Brinker a kidney punch: She had a lump in her breast that was cancerous. Knowing that her sexuality was not tied to her bra size, she screamed at her doctor, "I want them both off today! Get them off me!" She survived her ordeal; its side effects were weakness, baldness, and a renewed effort to find the cure. She was on the cusp of running, literally, into her eureka.

Nancy Brinker's eureka moment came one day while she was jogging. As she ran, she envisioned hundreds of women running for the cure, in a unique type of fund-raiser. They would come from all walks of life, united by a common cause, and their sponsors would be friends and family.

Such a race had never been organized before, and everyone told Brinker it would fail. However, on the first Komen Race for the Cure, on a drizzly Dallas day, eight hundred people showed up.

Within twenty years, the organization was sponsoring more than one hundred races annually, with more than a million participants. Donations pledged to the races have made $1 billion. The ubiquitous color of the organization is pink, manifested in the race with pink caps, pink T-shirts, and pink ribbons.

Nancy Brinker has devoted her life to keeping the deathbed promise she made to her big sister, and she will not stop until she has crossed the finish line: the demise of Susan's killer. The Goodman sisters' lives honored their mother's mantra, *Tikkun olam* ("Fix what is wrong with the world").

- In 2008, *Time* magazine included Nancy Brinker's name on its list of the 100 Most Influential People in the World.
- During Nancy's tenure as the ambassador to Budapest, she organized a cancer event in which hundreds of women marched along Chain Bridge, illuminated with pink lights.

- In 2007, for its twenty-fifth anniversary, the foundation launched an edgy campaign. On its T-shirts was the caption: "If you're going to stare at my breasts, you could at least donate a dollar to save them."

Eureka #38
(1983)

American tourists return from Italy with a variety of mementos: Materialistic people bring home Versace; amorous people bring home memories of *amore*; epicures bring home expanded waists. However, one pilgrim came back with a eureka that made him a modern Midas, and his stepdaughter's visage became recognizable throughout the world.

In the 1950s, Howard Schultz grew up in Bay View Houses, which, notwithstanding its exotic name, was anything but. When his father, Fred, broke his leg at work, his company provided no benefits, and the family lost its battle to make ends meet. Howard later recalled, "I saw the plight of a working-class family. I saw the fracturing of the American dream firsthand at the age of seven. That memory scarred me." An athletic scholarship served as his exit visa, and he became the first person in his family to graduate from college. Howard escaped the housing project, but its memory never left him.

In 1979, as the domestic manager for Hammarplast, a Swedish company, his interest was piqued when one small company was purchasing more of his drip coffeemakers than even Macy's. Intrigued, he paid it a visit and was to forever alter the palate, and the lexicon, of America.

The retailer was located in the historic Pike Place Market in Seattle. There he beheld a treasure trove of java: There were bins from Sumatra, Kenya, Ethiopia, and Costa Rica. This proved a revelation; in that era, most people thought coffee originated in a can. He was equally smitten with the care the store's owners put into roasting their beans, which were sold for home percolation. Howard recalls of that first visit, "I stepped inside and saw what looked like a temple for the worship of coffee.... It was my Mecca. I had arrived."

The coffee connoisseurs, who spoke of their product with the reverence generally reserved for fine wine, were more than happy to tell the interested young man the history of their company. The founder of their store was Alfred Peet, a Dutchman who did for coffee what Sir Walter Raleigh did for tobacco. In 1966, Peet opened a small store called Peet's Coffee and Tea in Berkeley.

A visitor and convert to the brew was Gordon Bower, who decided to open a similar store in Seattle. He convinced two of his friends, Jerry Baldwin (an English teacher) and Zev Siegel (a history teacher), to join him in the java venture. Gordon wanted to call his store Pequod, after the ship in *Moby-Dick*. However, it was vetoed with the comment that no one was going to want to buy beans from a store called *Pee-quod*. They also did not want to name it after the title of the novel (for obvious reasons). After further brainstorming, they decided to christen their establishment after Melville's first mate, Starbuck, a character who was constantly swilling coffee. Its logo was a brown-hued, sixteenth-century Norse woodcut of a bare-breasted, split-tailed mermaid, which the store's founders felt would be as seductive as the brew itself. On the flight back to New York City, Howard Schultz pushed away the airline coffee in disgust. Compared to what he had tasted in Seattle, he thought of it as swill.

When Howard arrived in New York, the siren's song of Starbucks would not let him go. He petitioned the owners to hire him as a manager; however, the three laid-back, Birkenstock-shod, older hippie trio had reservations about hiring a high-energy New Yorker into a company based on slow roasting. Finally, after a year, Howard's perseverance paid off; they agreed to have him on board.

Howard was ecstatic; his parents and friends less so. They thought it ridiculous to give up a $75,000 a year salary and company car to move three thousand miles away to join an unknown company. Howard and his wife, Sheri, packed up their Audi and drove west with Jonas, their hundred-pound golden retriever, in the backseat.

In 1983, when the company sent him to Italy for a housewares show, he discovered an espresso bar. He was entranced with the theater of the *barista* making the coffee, the animated Italians standing elbow to elbow gesturing over their drinks. It was there that Howard had his virgin café latte and his eureka moment: Starbucks needed to expand from selling beans and machines to serving exotic coffees in an inviting environment. His vision was to emulate the ambiance and espressos of Italy in the United States. He recalled in *Pour*

Your Heart into It, "The Italians had turned the drinking of coffee into a symphony, and it felt right. Starbucks was playing in the same hall, but we were playing without a string section." Once back in the States, Howard enthusiastically shared his vision for Starbucks, but was met with resistance. In 1985, Howard branched out on his own, which was a huge gamble because Sheri was pregnant.

Howard called his coffee house Il Giornale, the name of Italy's largest newspaper (which translates to "daily"), and had expanded his operation to three additional stores when he heard that Starbucks wanted to sell all six of its branches. Howard felt that he had to incorporate the two chains into one.

With the support of a six-foot-seven man who saw the same qualities in Schultz as he did in his own son, Bill Gates Sr. helped Howard achieve his dream by investing in it.

Schultz decided to forgo the name Il Giornale because it was difficult to pronounce. The logo also underwent a transformation from brown to green. The mermaid was made less seductive; her breasts were covered with flowing hair, and the split tail was camouflaged so that only the ends encircled the siren's face. The original is still displayed in Pike's Place.

In 1987, Starbucks had expanded to thirty stores, and the Schultz family had grown to include two children. Then came the phone call every child dreads: Howard's father was about to succumb to cancer.

When he visited his father, Howard held his hand and recalled when his dad had taken him to the Yankees game to see his idol, Mickey Mantle. In was then that Howard let go of his sense of what his father had not been able to achieve and to concentrate on what he had. He also realized that in some measure his father's financial failure had been instrumental in his own success. When an interviewer asked the 354th richest American what his most treasured possession was, he replied, "My memories." His statement proves his emotional IQ is equivalent to his business acumen.

Fred Schultz's death changed Starbucks because his son decided that he would no longer treat his employees the way his father had been treated; instead, he wanted "to build a company with soul." Howard arranged for health insurance packages, liberally including benefits for unmarried partners in committed relationships. In 1994, President Clinton was so impressed with the company's health-care policy that he invited Howard to the White House. After the interview, Howard called his mother and told her he was phoning from the White House. He only wished his father could have been there. However, as the catalyst for Starbucks benefits, in a sense, he was.

What originated as an epiphany in Italy has changed the landscape and lingo of America, and has become an integral part of the country's DNA. Howard took the coffee culture of Europe and put it on the corner of thousands of streets, from Birmingham to Bangkok. The star of Starbucks, Schultz, is now worth over 1 billion of those star-made bucks.

The coffee monolith has branched out to other arenas, producing its first movie, *Akeelah and the Bee*. It deals with a poor kid who, through a spelling contest, triumphs. One of the impressive words she can spell is "prestidigitation," which means "skill in pulling off illusions." It is an apt metaphor for Howard Schultz, who, through his epiphany, turned an ordinary beverage into an extraordinary empire.

Howard says he has plans to have at least 10,000 North American stores and 15,000 overseas. How big can the man from the Brooklyn projects dream? In barista lingo: Venti.

- In July 1993, the month of Schultz's fortieth birthday, his picture appeared on the cover of *Fortune* magazine. Its caption: "Howard Schultz's Starbucks grinds coffee into gold." He had become the twentieth-century's version of an alchemist.
- The company has 40 million customers a week.
- Schultz is a significant stakeholder in Jamba Juice.
- Schultz sold the NBA's Seattle SuperSonics for $350 million.

Eureka #39
(1994)

Words carry connotations. To some, "Amazon" conjures up an exotic locale; to others, a sisterhood of strong women; to even others, a superheroine with spandex shorts. However, in the waning years of the twentieth century, the term was to don another mantle because of a eureka moment.

In Albuquerque in 1964, seventeen-year-old Jacklyn Gise Jorgenson, a teenage bank teller, gave birth to Jeffrey Preston; her ill-fated marriage lasted a year. Her second husband was Miguel Bezos, who had fled from Cuba when he was a teenager. With him she found happiness; he legally adopted her son, and they had two children together.

From a young age, Jeffrey proved to have an intellect usually associated with prodigies. At three, weary of his sleeping arrangement, he located a screwdriver and disassembled his crib. A few years later, he rigged an electric alarm to prevent his siblings from entering his room. At age fourteen, he tried, unsuccessfully, to build a hovercraft out of a vacuum cleaner.

Jeffrey recalls it wasn't until he was ten that he discovered Miguel was not his biological father. His parents' fears about how he would take the news proved unfounded. He said what did make him cry at the time was being told he needed to start wearing glasses.

In high school, Jeffrey met his first love: computers. And once he had set his sights on being his school's valedictorian, every other student knew second place was all they could aspire to. He graduated from Princeton University summa cum laude with a degree in computer science and electrical engineering.

After graduation, Jeff headed to Wall Street. He obtained a position at the hedge fund D. E. Shaw, a firm specializing in the application of computer science to the stock market. Jeff rose quickly in the ranks and was soon promoted to senior vice president, the youngest person ever to attain the position in the company's history.

Once he had carved out his financial security with a six-figure salary, he turned to his personal life, asking friends to set him up on some blind dates. He explained, "I'm not the kind of person where women say, 'Oh, look how great he is' a half hour after meeting me. I'm kind of goofy, and I'm not ah-ha-ha-ha-ha-ha!—the kind of thing where people are going to say about me, 'Oh my God, this is what I've been looking for!'"

Jeff ended up falling in love with fellow Princeton graduate and coworker McKenzie Tuttle. Before working at Shaw, she had followed her literary love by obtaining a position as an assistant to Toni Morrison. The couple ended up marrying.

In 1994, while surfing the web in search of new ventures for D. E. Shaw, he realized a staggering statistic: Internet use was growing by 2,300 percent a year. This statistic led to his eureka moment: The real investment was in the Net itself.

He raced to Shaw's president with his revelation, but his boss was unconvinced. Jeff decided to venture into erstwhile unchartered waters, starting up an e-commerce venture. Now that he had the brainstorm, he had to come up with a product; in the end, he determined his ticket was books. He based his choice on the fact that the most popular means of selling, other than stores, was the mail-order catalog. However, he saw the Internet as superior because it could carry millions of titles, while the catalog could at most carry a few hundred because of postal weight. He further figured his business would rival that of traditional bookstores; even the largest of them could only stock a few thousand titles, a mere fraction of what could be offered in a virtual one. Perhaps he was further inspired by the fact that his wife was a literature lover.

The die was cast; Jeff Bezos was ready to cross his electronic Rubicon. Bezos passed up a fat bonus check and ignored the naysayers who said he was mad to abandon substance for shadow. He later explained to *Time*, "When I'm eighty, am I going to regret leaving Wall Street? No. Will I regret missing the beginning of the Internet? Yes." Jeff and McKenzie left New York City, hitching their wagon to the web and heading west; for an online bookseller, it would be ridiculous to set up shop in an expensive New York City ZIP code. While McKenzie drove their Chevy Blazer and conversed with their golden retriever, Jeff crunched numbers. The end of the odyssey was Seattle, where they rented a two-bedroom house and turned its garage into what they hailed as "the world's largest bookstore."

Jeff set up stations on tables he made out of doors from Home Depot. He rigged each of them so that a bell would ring every time there was a sale. He then went on endless sales pitches to lure investors. One of these sales pitches was to his parents, whose first question was, "What's the Internet?" After he explained, they invested their life savings of $300,000. Jackie explained they were not investing in the business; they were investing in Jeff.

The next step was for Bezos to christen his brainchild. Jeff thought of the name Cadabra, as a shortened version of "Abracadabra." However, this was shelved when his lawyer misheard it and replied, "Cadaver! Why would you want to call your company after a corpse?" Bezos changed it to Amazon, after one of the world's most famous rivers. An added incentive for the choice was that, at the time, Yahoo! was listing its sites in alphabetical order.

The following year, in 1995, Amazon.com opened its virtual doors, offering a million titles. Soon the bell that rang when there was a sale was dismantled because there was too much ringing. As sales grew and grew, the everentrepreneurial Bezos kept fine-tuning his creation, implementing novel ideas such as one-click shopping and email verification. He also developed a way to make armchair shopping as interactive as it was easy: Customers could view first pages, similar books, and bestsellers. The online reviews became a form of chatting, making it even more personal than solitary browsing in a traditional bookstore. In this fashion, the reviews provided a sense of connectedness—exactly the opposite of the stereotypical view of the isolation and alienation of online shopping.

In the process, Jeff became one of the wealthiest people in the world; his parents' ROJ (return on Jeff) made them billionaires. He attributes his success to luck, claiming it couldn't have happened without "planetary alignment." However, success came to the goofy geek due to brilliance, hard work, and a eureka moment.

A quotation states "the business of America is business." Because of a eureka from a boy born on the wrong side of the tracks, the world has changed the way it does business. And, along the way, Jeff Bezos has become king of the Internet.

- Bezos is starting Blue Origin, which is a Seattle-based venture to create a reusable commercial spacecraft that will take paying passengers on suborbital flights.
- In a *Time* interview, Bezos cited his heroes as Thomas Edison and Walt Disney.
- Not content to merely revolutionize the way the world buys books, Jeff set out to alter the way we read them as well. In 2007, Amazon launched the Kindle (the name connotes ignition, as in the spark of knowledge), a handheld electronic reading device. Hundreds of books can be stored on the Kindle, and books can be downloaded instantly.
- Amazon.com shares jumped 40 percent on April 25 and 26 in 2007, which earned Bezos $1.8 billion in two days.

Eureka #40
(1998)

One common pet peeve is the late fee, a punishment levied by libraries, credit card companies, landlords, and parking authorities. Most people react to these with a gnashing of teeth; however, one man, because of his eureka moment, managed to eradicate them in one arena. And, in the process, he transformed American homes into something that was once the realm of the Jetsons.

Wilmot Hastings' father was a lawyer who served in the Nixon administration. He recalls, "One weekend when I was about twelve, my parents, sisters, and I were invited to Camp David, when the president wasn't there. We rode around in golf carts, had a tour, and I saw that President Nixon had a gold-colored toilet seat."

Hastings attended college in Maine, where he won a prize in mathematics, a subject whose abstractions he viewed "as beautiful and engaging."

As the child of privilege and private education, Hastings desired to give something back, so he joined the Marine

Corps Platoon Leaders Class. He spent the summer between his sophomore and junior years in a boot camp in Virginia. However, the experience was not a love connection. Hastings recalled, "I found myself questioning how we packed our backpacks and how we made our beds. My questioning wasn't particularly encouraged, and I realized I might be better off in the Peace Corps. I petitioned the recruiting office and left the Marines."

That was how the Bostonian Hastings found himself teaching math as a Peace Corps volunteer in Swaziland. He taught at a high school with eight hundred students in a rural part of the country. There was no electricity, and cooking was done with propane and wood. Corn was the staple of his diet, and his sleeping accommodations consisted of a cot in a thatched hut. He found the experience extremely gratifying, and it satisfied his twin need of having an adventure and providing assistance.

On his return, he enrolled in graduate school at Stanford to pursue a degree in computer science. What influenced him more than the school's "ivy" was California's palm trees. He viewed sunny Palo Alto as a dream compared to chilly New England. He told his parents he had "found nirvana" and knew the West was where his future, whatever it would hold, would lie.

After walking the roads of volunteer work and Ivy League education, Hastings (known by his middle name of Reed) was ready to tread the path of business. He started Pure Software, designed to troubleshoot computer programs. As it grew from 10 employees to 640, he found himself overwhelmed. He analyzed his situation with an analogy: "I was doing white-

PlanetChiropractic.com. www.planetc1.com/cgi-bin/n/v.cgi?c=1&id+1221 723732 (accessed June 1, 2009).

"History of Chiropractic." Academy of Upper Cervical Chiropractic Organizations Inc. www.aucco.org/history.html (accessed June 1, 2009).

"History of Chiropractic." AECC Chiropractic College. www.aecc.ac.uk/career/history/index.asp (accessed June 1, 2009).

"History of Chiropractic." Parkland Chiropractic and Healing Center. www.parklandchiropractic.com/Chiro/history.html (accessed June 1, 2009).

"The History of Chiropractic." The World Chiropractic Alliance. www.worldchiro practicalliance.org/consumer/history.htm (accessed June 1, 2009).

Keating Jr., Joseph. "A Hundred Years Ago in Chiropractic." April 20, 1998. Dynamic Chiropractic. www.chiroweb.com/archives/16/09/11.html (accessed June 1, 2009).

Palmer, Daniel David. "A Brief History of the Author and Chiropractic." Chiropractic's Discovery. http://chirobase.org/12Hx/discovery.html (accessed June 1, 2009).

Russell, Michael. "Chiropractor: History of Chiropractic." Ezine Articles. http://ezinearticles.com/?Chiropractor—History-of-Chiropractic&id=314882 (accessed June 1, 2009).

9. The Wright Brothers

Dixon-Engel, Tara, and Mike Jackson. *The Wright Brothers*. New York: Sterling Publishing, 2007.

Freedman, Russell. *The Wright Brothers*. New York: Holiday House, 1991.

10. Tour de France

Abt, Samuel. "Cycling: Tour de France Kicks Up Its Heels." Nov. 22, 2002. *New York Times*. www.nytimes.com/2002/11/22/sports/22iht-bike_ed3__0.html (accessed July 5, 2008).

Barnett, Kaye. "The History of the Tour de France." Bella Online. www.bella online.com/articles/art11240.asp (accessed July 5, 2008).

Fotheringham, Alasdair. "Cycling: France Seeks Heroes to Rekindle Glories of the Past." June 20, 2003. *The Independent.* www.independent.co.uk/sport/general/cycling-france-seeks-heroes-to-rekindle-glories-of-the-past-542321.html (accessed July 5, 2008).

"Geo Lefevre." 2009. Wikipedia. http://en.wikipedia.org/wiki/Geo_Lefevre.

"J'accuse." Citizendia. www.hickoksports.com/history/tourdefrance.shtml.

"The Origins of the Tour de France." Jan. 26, 2008. Cycling Info. http://cyclinginfo .co.uk/blog/procycling/the-origins-of-the-tour-de-france (accessed July 5, 2008).

Pickert, Kate. "A Brief History Of: The Tour de France." July 3, 2008. *Time*. www.time.com/time/printout/0,8816,1820136,00.html (accessed July 5, 2008).

"Tour de France." 2009. Wikipedia. http://en.wikipedia.org/wiki/Tour_de_france.

"Tour de France." Hickok Sports. www.hickoksports.com/history/tourde france.shtml (accessed July 5, 2008).

11. Planned Parenthood

Katz, Esther. "Margaret Sanger." Feb. 2000. American National Biography Online. www.anb.org/articles/15/15-00598-print.html (accessed Feb. 22, 2009).

"Margaret Sanger." 1996. Gale Research. www.gale.cengage.com/free_resources/whm/bio/sanger_m.htm (accessed Feb. 17, 2009).

12. *Reader's Digest*

"Hoover's Profile: The Reader's Digest Association Inc." Answers.com. www.answers.com/topic/reader-s-digest (accessed Dec. 30, 2008).

Lingeman, Richard. "Processed in Pleasantville." Aug. 22, 1993. *New York Times*. www.nytimes.com/1993/08/22/books/processed-in-pleasantville.html?page wanted=all (accessed Dec. 30, 2008).

Wallace, Irving, and David Wallechinsky. "History of Reader's Digest Magazine." 1981. www.trivia-library.com/b/history-of-readers-digest-magazine-part-2 .htm (accessed Dec. 30, 2008).

13. Mount Rushmore

Buckingham, Matthew. "The Six Grandfathers, Paha Sapa, in the Year 502,002 C.E." *Cabinet*. www.cabinetmagazine.org/issues/7/sixgrandfathers.php (accessed Oct. 31, 2008).

"Mount Rushmore." *American Experience*. www.pbs.org/wgbh/amex/rushmore/peopleevents/e_contest.html (accessed Oct. 31, 2008).

"Mount Rushmore." 2009. Wikipedia. http://en.wikipedia.org/wiki/Mt_rush more.

14. Winnie-the-Pooh

"A. A. Milne." 2009. Wikipedia. http://en.wikipedia.org/wiki/A._A._Milne.

"Alan Alexander Milne, Author." Pooh Corner. www.poohcorner.com/Alan -Alexander-Milne-Author.html (accessed April 30, 2009).

"Christopher Robin Milne." www.lair2000.net/Pooh_Corner/pooh_characters/ChrisRobin.html (accessed May 1, 2008).

Harris, Angela. "A. A. Milne: Creator of One of the World's Most Beloved Characters, Winnie the Pooh." May 30, 2007. Associated Content. www.associated

content.com/article/256901/a_a_milne_creator_of_one_of_the_worlds
.html?cat=38 (accessed April 30, 2009).

Milne, James. "The Author." June 16, 2005. Pooh Corner. www.pooh-corner
.org/milne.shtml (accessed April 30, 2009).

"Winnie-the-Pooh." 2009. Wikipedia. http://en.wikipedia.org/wiki/Winnie
-the-Pooh.

"Winnie the Pooh Biography." Who2? www.who2.com/winniethepooh.html.

15. Disney

"Biography for Walt Disney." The Internet Movie Database. www.imdb.com/
name/nm0000370/bio.

Churchwell, Sarah. "The Animated Walt Disney." Aug. 15, 2007. *Times Online: The
Times Literary Supplement.* http://tls.timesonline.co.uk/article/0,,25336
-2648703,00.html (accessed Dec. 4, 2008).

Crowther, Bosley. "Walt Disney Biography." Biography.com. www.biography.com
/articles/Walt-Disney-9275533?part=0 (accessed Dec. 4, 2008).

"Disneyland Park (Anaheim)." 2008. Wikipedia. http://en.wikipedia.org/wiki/
Disneyland_park.

"The Final Resting Place of Walt Disney." www.hollywoodusa.co.uk/glendale
obituaries/waltdisney.htm (accessed Dec. 3, 2008).

Langer, Mark. "Walt Disney." Feb. 2000. *American National Biography Online.*
www.anb.org/articles/18/18-00309.html (accessed Dec. 5, 2008).

Malloy, Betsy. "Disneyland History: An Overview of Disneyland History."
About.com. http://gocalifornia.about.com/od/cadisneyland/a/history
.htm (accessed Nov. 25, 2008).

Schuman, Jeff. "The History of Disneyland." April 4, 2007. Associated Content.
www.associatedcontent.com/article/192782/the_history_of_disneyland
.html?cat=16 (accessed Dec. 3, 2008).

"Walt Disney." Oct. 12, 2004. Famous People. www.famouspeople.co.uk/w/walt
disney.html (accessed Dec. 4, 2008).

"Walt Disney." Ron & Marie's Disney Trivia. www.disneytrivia.net/walt_bio.php
(accessed Dec. 4, 2008).

16. Grauman's Chinese Theatre

Endres, Stacey, and Robert Cushman. *Hollywood at Your Feet.* Beverly Hills:
Pomegranate Press, 1992.

Katzizkidz. "Sid Grauman." Find a Grave. www.findagrave.com/cgi-bin/fg.cgi?
page=gr&GRid=413 (accessed Sept. 29, 2009).

Teicholz, Tom. "Happy Birthday, Mr. Grauman." www.thewrap.com/blog-entry/
1874 (accessed Sept. 20, 2009).

17. Dr. Seuss

Brinkley, Douglas. "Laughter's Perennial at the Doctor's Seussentennial." March 2, 2004. *New York Times*. www.nytimes.com/2004/03/02/books/02SEUS.html (accessed Sept. 13, 2008).

"Dr. Seuss." 2008. Wikipedia. http://en.wikipedia.org/wiki/Dr._Seuss.

18. Penguin Books

"About Penguin: Company History." Penguin. www.penguin.co.uk/static/cs/uk/0/aboutus/history.html (accessed Oct. 13, 2008).

"Being Able to Pick Up a Penguin en Route Home." April 27, 2005. *Huddersfield Daily Examiner*. www.examiner.co.uk/news/tm_objectid=15451116&method=full&siteid=50060&headline=-being-able-to-pick-up-a-penguin-en-route-home—name_page.html (accessed Oct. 14, 2008).

"The Man Who Was Penguin." May 1, 2005. *The Independent*. www.independent.co.uk/arts-entertainment/books/features/the-man-who-was-penguin-490617.html (accessed Oct. 14, 2008).

Morpurgo, Clare. "Allen Lane and His Foundation." 2006. Allen Lane Foundation. www.allenlane.org.uk/2006_lecture.htm (accessed Oct. 13, 2008).

Morpurgo, Horatio. "Lady Chatterley's Defendant: Allen Lane and the Paperback Revolution." Sept. 2008. Three Monkeys Online. www.threemonkeysonline.com/als_page2/allen_lane_lady_chatterley.html.

"Penguin Books." NationMaster.com. www.statemaster.com/encyclopedia/Penguin-Books.

"Penguin Books: History." Books and Writers. www.booksandwriters.co.uk/writer/P/penguin-books—history.asp.

Sebastian, Pradeep. "It Is a Penguin Classic, Boss!" *The Hindu*. www.thehindu.com/thehindu/lr/2005/12/04/stories/2005120400230500.htm (accessed Oct. 19, 2008).

19. Alcoholics Anonymous

"Alcoholics Anonymous." Boston University Theology Library. http://sthweb.bu.edu/archives/index.php?option=com_awiki&view=mediawiki&article=Alcoholics_Anonymous.

Baer, Adam. "AA Founder Longed to Be a Regular Guy." March 7, 2004. *San Francisco Chronicle*. www.sfgate.com/cgi-bin/article.cgi?file=/chronicle/archive/2004/03/07/RVGRF5A39Q1.DTL (accessed June 14, 2008).

Borchert, Bill. "About the Book." The Lois Wilson Story. www.theloiswilsonstory.com/ (accessed June 14, 2008).

Cheever, Susan. "The Healer." June 14, 1999. *Time*. www.time.com/time/printout/0,8816,991266,00.html (accessed June 14, 2008).

Edmeades, Baz. "Alcoholics Anonymous Celebrates Its 150th Year." Aug. 1985.

Saturday Evening Post. http://silkworth.net/magazine_newspaper/
saturday_evening_post_aug_1985.html (accessed June 14, 2008).

English, Rich. "The Dry Piper." *Modern Drunkard Magazine.* www.modern
drunkardmagazine.com/issues/01-05/0105-dry-piper.htm (accessed June
14, 2008).

"History of Alcoholics Anonymous." 2008. Wikipedia. http://en.wikipedia.org/
wiki/History_of_Alcoholics_Anonymous.

Kammen, Michael. "Found in a Bottle." March 21, 2004. *New York Times: Books.*
www.nytimes.com/2004/03/21/books/found-in-a-bottle.html (accessed
June 15, 2008).

"Lois Wilson (activist)." 2008. Wikipedia. http://en.wikipedia.org/wiki/Lois_
Wilson_(activist).

"Timeline of Events Related to AA." www.aaprovidencepoint.com/aatimeline
.htm (accessed June 15, 2008).

20. *Casablanca*

"Murray Burnett." 2008. Wikipedia. http://en.wikipedia.org/wiki/Murray_
Burnett.

Murray, Janet H. "Here's Looking at Casablanca." Oct. 2005. *Humanities.*
www.neh.gov/news/humanities/2005-09/casablanca.html.

"Trivia for Casablanca (1942)." The Internet Movie Database.
www.imdb.com/title/tt0034583/trivia (accessed May 21, 2008).

21. *Curious George*

"Curious George History." FunToCollect.com. www.funtocollect.com/curhis
.html (accessed June 20, 2008)

22. Wonder Woman

"Biography for William M. Marston." The Internet Movie Database. www.imdb
.com/name/nm0551376/bio.

"Elizabeth H. Marston, Inspiration for Wonder Woman, 100." April 3, 1993. *New
York Times.* www.nytimes.com/1993/04/03/obituaries/elizabeth-h-marston
-inspiration-for-wonder-woman-100.html (accessed June 22, 2008).

"Elizabeth Holloway Marston." 2008. Wikipedia. http://en.wikipedia.org/wiki/
Elizabeth_Holloway_Marston.

Kurtzman, Harvey. "The First One to Wonder About a Wonder Woman." 2005.
WilliamMoultonMarston.com. www.geocities.com/toonpro/domains/
comiccreators/com_marston (accessed June 22, 2008).

Lalumiere, Claude. "Bound Wonder." Feb. 2001. *January Magazine.* http://january
magazine.com/artcult/wonderwoman.html (accessed June 21, 2008).

Malcolm, Andrew. "Our Towns; She's Behind the Match for That Man of Steel." Feb. 18, 1992. *New York Times*. www.nytimes.com/1992/02/18/nyregion/our -towns-she-s-behind-the-match-for-that-man-of-steel.html (accessed June 22, 2008).

Pereira, K. L. "Female Bonding." 2006. Hot and Bothered. http://bitchmagazine .org/article/female-bonding (accessed June 22, 2008).

Shefcyk, Allison. "Wonder Woman: A MoHo?" March 10, 2006. *Mount Holyoke News*. http://media.www.themhnews.com/media/storage/paper999/news /2006/03/10/Features/Wonder.Woman.A.Moho-1684418.shtml (accessed June 22, 2008).

SlackerDan. "Five Secondary but Still Famous Superhero Origins." May 30, 2008. Purple Slinky. http://purpleslinky.com/offbeat/five-secondary-but-still -famous-superhero-origins (accessed June 22, 2008).

Tiff. "What Is the Origin of Wonder Woman?" 2006. Answer Bag. www.answer bag.com/q_view/51432.

Tipton, Scott. "Enter Diana." April 28, 2004. Comics 101. http://quickstopenter tainment.com/comics101/62.html (accessed June 22, 2008).

"William Moulton Marston." 2008. Wikipedia. http://en.wikipedia.org/wiki/ William_Moulton_Marston.

"Wonder Woman." 2008. Wikipedia. http://en.wikipedia.org/wiki/Wonder_ Woman.

"Wonder Woman." www.uky.edu/Projects/Chemcomics/html/ww_21_cov.html.

23. Slinky

"It's Slinky, It's Slinky." Feb. 11, 2001. CNN. http://archives.cnn.com/2001/US/02 /10/slinky.story/ (accessed May 20, 2008).

"Slinky History." July 20, 2005. The Great Idea Finder. www.ideafinder.com/ history/inventions/slinky.htm (accessed May 20, 2008).

24. Club Med

"Club Med." 2008. Wikipedia. http://en.wikipedia.org/wiki/Club_Med.

"Club Med—The Beginnings." Club Med. http://travelpartner.clubmed.com.au/ ph_dd/3216_events.php?cid=41560 (accessed Jan. 31, 2009).

"Club Mediterranée S.A." FundingUniverse. www.fundinguniverse.com/company -histories/Club-Mediterraneacute;e-SA-Company-History.html (accessed Jan. 27, 2009).

"Gilbert Trigano." Feb. 5, 2001. *Telegraph*. www.telegraph.co.uk/news/obituaries /1321129/Gilbert-Trigano.html (accessed Jan. 31, 2009).

"Gilbert Trigano." Babson College. www3.babson.edu/ESHIP/outreach-events/ Gilbert-Trigano.cfm (accessed Jan. 27, 2009).

Lichfield, John. "Gilbert Trigano." Feb. 7, 2001. *Independent.* www.independent
.co.uk/news/obituaries/gilbert-trigano-728840.html (accessed Jan. 31, 2009).

Spano, Susan. "Club Med Rolls on Through Love, War and Trends Galore." Dec.
11, 2005. *Los Angeles Times.* www.latimes.com/travel/la-tr-spano11dec11,1,
7967706.column (accessed Jan. 27, 2009).

25. Guinness World Records

Altman, Alex. "Guinness World Records." Nov. 14, 2008. *Time.* www.time.com/
time/arts/article/0,8599,1859037,00.html (accessed Dec. 17, 2008).

Asiado, Tel. "Guinness World Records: Beginnings." Suite101.com. http://
historicalresources.suite101.com/article.cfm/guinness_world_records
_beginnings (accessed Dec. 17, 2008).

Connell, Nick. "The History of Guinness World Records." Nov. 16, 2007. *The
Yorker.* www.theyorker.co.uk/news/theknow/795 (accessed Dec. 17, 2008).

"Guinness Book of Records." 2008. Wikipedia. http://en.wikipedia.org/wiki/
Guinness_Book_of_Records.

Stoffman, Judy. "Guinness Book's Big Boy." Aug. 20, 2006. TheStar.com.
www.thestar.com/printArticle/95323 (accessed Dec. 17, 2008).

Watson, Bruce. "World's Unlikeliest Bestseller." Aug. 2005. *Smithsonian.*
www.smithsonianmag.com/science-nature/bestseller.html (accessed Dec.
17, 2008).

26. Sweet'N Low

Eng, Christina. "A Bittersweet Family History." April 23, 2006. *San Francisco
Chronicle.* http://sfgate.info/cgi-bin/article.cgi?f=/c/a/2006/04/23/RVGGHI
8MTC1.DTL&hw=patriarch&sn=302&sc=303 (accessed Oct. 28, 2008).

Hamill, Denis. "Salt-of-the-Earth Guy Was Sweet, Too." April 12, 1996. *Daily
News.* www.nydailynews.com/archives/ny_local/1996/04/12/1996-04-12_
salt-of-the-earth_guy_was_sw.html (accessed Oct. 28, 2008).

Kuntzman, Gersh. "Sugar Substitute . . . and Spice." April 22, 2006. *Brooklyn
Paper.* www.brooklynpaper.com/stories/29/16/29_16sweetandlow.html
(accessed Oct. 28, 2008).

27. Barbie

"Barbie." 2008. Wikipedia. http://en.wikipedia.org/wiki/Barbie_doll.

"The Barbie Doll Story." Raving Toy Maniac. www.toymania.com/news/
messages/barbiehistory.shtml (accessed May 12, 2008).

"Barbie Dolls." History of Toys. www.history.com/content/toys/toys-games
(accessed May 12, 2008).

"Fascinating Facts About the Barbie Doll." July 22, 2007. Associated Content.
www.associatedcontent.com/article/313527/fascinating_facts_about_the
_barbie.html?cat=37 (accessed May 12, 2008).

"Ruth Handler." 1999. Inventor of the Week. http://web.mit.edu/invent/iow/
handler.html (accessed May 12, 2008).

Steele-Carlin, Sherril. "Barbie: History of a Living Doll." Rewind the Fifties.
www.loti.com/barbie_mattel_1959.htm (accessed May 12, 2008).

Wolf, Erica. "Barbie: The Early History." 2000. www.honors.umd.edu/HONR269J/
projects/wolf.html (accessed May 12, 2008).

28. Amnesty International

"Amnesty International." 2008. Wikipedia. http://en.wikipedia.org/wiki/
Amnesty_International.

Archer, Peter. "Peter Benenson." Feb. 28, 2005. *Guardian.* www.guardian.co.uk/
news/2005/feb/28/guardianobituaries.humanrights (accessed Dec. 26,
2008).

Blom-Cooper, Louis. "Peter Benenson." Dec. 4, 2005. *Observer.* www.guardian.co
.uk/theobserver/2005/dec/04/features.magazine97 (accessed Dec. 25, 2008).

O'Shaughnessy, Hugh. "Peter Benenson." Feb. 28, 2005. *Independent.*
www.independent.co.uk/news/obituaries/peter-benenson-485186.html
(accessed Dec. 26, 2008).

"Peter Benenson." Feb. 28, 2005. *Telegraph.* www.telegraph.co.uk/news/obit
uaries/1484539/Peter-Benenson.html (accessed Dec. 26, 2008).

"Peter Benenson." March 11, 2005. MoreOrLess. www.moreorless.au.com/heroes
/benenson.html (accessed July 25, 2008).

"Peter Benenson." Amnesty International. www2.amnesty.se/hem.nsf/peter
benensonbgr?OpenPage (accessed Dec. 26, 2008).

29. Weight Watchers

France, Louise. "The Woman Who Taught the World to Slim." Jan. 13, 2008.
Observer. www.guardian.co.uk/lifeandstyle/2008/jan/13/healthandwell
being.features2 (accessed June 19, 2009).

"Jean Nidetch, Benefactor." University of Nevada, Las Vegas. http://womens
center.unlv.edu/benefactor.htm (accessed June 19, 2009).

30. Mary Kay

Allen, Scott. "Mary Kay Ash: Most Outstanding Woman in Business in the 20th
Century." About.com: Entrepreneurs. http://entrepreneurs.about.com/od/
famousentrepreneurs/p/marykayash.htm (accessed Jan. 3, 2009).

Gavenas, Mary Lisa. "Mary Kay Ash." 2008. American National Biography Online.
www.anb.org/articles/10/10-02284.html (accessed Jan. 3, 2009).

"Mary Kay." 2009. Wikipedia. http://en.wikipedia.org/wiki/Mary_Kay.

"Mary Kay Ash." 1999. Gale Research. www.novelguide.com/a/discover/bls_01/
bls_01_00020.html (accessed Jan. 3, 2009).

"Mary Kay Ash." Answers.com. www.answers.com/topic/mary-kay-ash (accessed Jan. 3, 2009).

"Mary Kay Ash Biography." 2006. A&E Television. www.biography.com/articles/ Mary-Kay-Ash-197044 (accessed Jan. 3, 2009).

"Mary Kay Ash Biography." Notable Biographies. www.notablebiographies.com/ An-Ba/Ash-Mary-Kay.html (accessed Jan. 3, 2009).

"Mary Kay, Inc." Funding Universe. www.fundinguniverse.com/company -histories/Mary-Kay-Inc-Company-History.html (accessed Jan. 3, 2009).

McFarland, John. "Mary Kay Ash, 83, Kept Cosmetics Line in the 'Pink.'" Nov. 27, 2001. *Star*. www.thestar.com/obituary/htom/article/107672 (accessed Jan. 3, 2009).

Nemy, Enid. "Mary Kay Ash, Who Built a Cosmetic Empire and Adored Pink, Is Dead at 83." Nov. 23, 2001. *New York Times*. www.nytimes.com/2001/11/23/ business/mary-kay-ash-who-built-a-cosmetics-empire-and-adored-pink-is -dead-at-83.html (accessed Jan. 3, 2009).

"Women Leaders: Mary Kay Ash." The Leadership Resource. www.theleadership resource.com/WomenLeaders04.php (accessed Jan. 3, 2009).

31. Jeopardy!

"The Art Fleming Years." 2008. www.geocities.com/artflemingjeopardy/64 history.html.

Associated Press. "Merv Griffin, 82, Dies of Prostate Cancer." Aug. 12, 2007. MSNBC. www.msnbc.msn.com/id/20236685 (accessed June 24, 2008).

Bernstein, Adam. "Merv Griffin; TV Host, Game-Show Creator." Aug. 13, 2007. *Washington Post*. www.washingtonpost.com/wp-dyn/content/article/2007/ 08/12/AR2007081200453.html.

Cosgrove-Mather, Bootie. "Merv Griffin's Good Life." March 28, 2003. CBS News. www.cbsnews.com/stories/2003/03/28/print/main546604.shtml (accessed June 24, 2008).

Dickensheets, Scott. "What I've Learned: Merv Griffin." Aug.13, 2007. *Esquire*. www.esquire.com/features/what-ive-learned/ESQ0906WIL_244 (accessed June 24, 2008).

"Jeopardy!" 2009. Wikipedia. http://en.wikipedia.org/wiki/Jeopardy.

"Merv Griffin." 2009. Wikipedia. http://en.wikipedia.org/wiki/Merv_Griffin.

Thomas, Bob. "Merv Griffin Dies from Cancer at 82." Aug. 13, 2007. *San Francisco Chronicle*. www.sfgate.com/cgi-bin/article.cgi?f=/n/a/2007/08/13/entertain ment/e065103D75.DTL (accessed June 24, 2008).

32. Roots

"Alex Haley." 2009. Gale Research. www.gale.cengage.com/free_resources/bhm/ bio/haley_a.htm (accessed Feb. 8, 2009).

"Alex Haley." *Tennessee Online*. www.vic.com/tnchron/class/Ahaley.htm (accessed Feb. 8, 2009).

"Alex Haley." 2009. Wikipedia. http://en.wikipedia.org/wiki/Alex_Haley.

Marius, Richard. "Alex Murray Palmer Haley." *The Tennessee Encyclopedia of History and Culture*. http://tennesseeencyclopedia.net/imagegallery.php?Entry ID=H004 (accessed Feb. 8, 2009).

"Roots: The Saga of an American Family." Wikipedia. 2009. http://en.wikipedia .org/wiki/Roots:_The_Saga_of_an_American_Family (accessed Feb. 8, 2009).

33. Kwanzaa

"Kwanzaa." 2008. Wikipedia. http://en.wikipedia.org/wiki/Kwanzaa.

"Ron Karenga." 2009. Wikipedia. http://en.wikipedia.org/wiki/Maulana_Karenga.

"Ron Karenga." Fact-Archive.com. http://www.fact-archive.com/encyclopedia/ Maulana_Karenga (accessed Feb. 4, 2009).

34. Special Olympics

"Eunice Kennedy Shriver." 2004. NovelGuide. www.novelguide.com/a/discover/ nspf_03/nspf_03_00516.html (accessed Nov. 6, 2008).

"Eunice Kennedy Shriver." NationMaster. www.nationmaster.com/encyclopedia/ Eunice-Kennedy-Shriver (accessed Nov. 7, 2008).

"Eunice Kennedy Shriver." NetGlimse. www.netglimse.com/celebs/pages/eunice _kennedy_shriver/index.shtml (accessed Nov. 6, 2008).

"Eunice Kennedy Shriver: Someone Believes." http://sports.jrank.org/pages/4419/ Shriver-Eunice-Kennedy-Someone-Believes.html (accessed Nov. 7, 2008).

"History." Special Olympics. www.somena.org/showpage.aspx?PID=15 (accessed Nov. 6, 2008).

McCallum, Jack. "In Praise of the Founder of the Special Olympics." Nov. 28, 2007. *Sports Illustrated*. http://sportsillustrated.cnn.com/2007/magazine/specials/ sportsman/2007/11/07/mccallum.kennedy/index.html (accessed Nov. 6, 2008).

Meyer, Jennifer. "Special Olympics." Learning to Give. http://learningtogive.org/ papers/paper184.html.

Mitchell, Sandy. "Eunice Shriver: Mother of the Special Olympics." May 10, 2008. EveryJoe.com. www.everyjoe.com/articles/eunice-shriver-mother-of-the -special-olympics-92 (accessed Nov. 6, 2008).

P., Rachel. "Eunice Kennedy Shriver." www.op97.k12.il.us/curriculum/cafe/ zonta/rachelP.html (accessed Nov. 6, 2008).

"Sargent Shriver." 2008. Wikipedia. http://en.wikipedia.org/wiki/Sargent_ Shriver.

"Special Olympics." 2008. Wikipedia. http://en.wikipedia.org/wiki/Special_ Olympics.

"Special Olympics." TripAtlas.com. http://tripatlas.com/Special_Olympics.
Suarez, Ray. "The Beginnings of a Movement." July 12, 2006. *Online NewsHour.*
   www.pbs.org/newshour/bb/sports/july-dec06/shriver_07-12.html (accessed
   Nov. 6, 2008).

35. Hard Rock Café

"Hard Rock Cafe." 2008. Wikipedia. http://en.wikipedia.org/wiki/Hard_Rock_Cafe.
"Hard Rock Café." NovelGuide. www.novelguide.com/a/discover/cps_01/cps_01
   _00131.html (accessed Jan. 12, 2009).
"Hard Rock Café International, Inc." FundingUniverse. www.fundinguniverse
   .com/company-histories/Hard-Rock-Cafe-International-Inc-Company
   -History.html (accessed Jan. 11, 2009).
Martin, Richard. "Peter Morton & Isaac Tigrett." Feb. 1996. BNET. http://find
   articles.com/p/articles/mi_m3190/is_nSPEISS_v30/ai_18091893 (accessed
   Jan. 11, 2009).

36. People for the Ethical Treatment of Animals

"Ingrid Newkirk." 2008. Wikipedia. http://en.wikipedia.org/wiki/Ingrid_Newkirk.
"People for the Ethical Treatment of Animals." 2008. Wikipedia. http://en
   .wikipedia.org/wiki/People_for_the_Ethical_Treatment_of_Animals.
"People for the Ethical Treatment of Animals." Answers.com. www.answers.com/
   topic/people-for-the-ethical-treatment-of-animals (accessed July 16, 2008).

37. Race for the Cure

"Nancy Brinker." 2008. Wikipedia. http://en.wikipedia.org/wiki/Nancy_Brinker.
"Nancy Brinker Biography." NotableBiographies.com. www.notablebiographies
   .com/newsmakers2/2007-A-Co/Brinker-Nancy.html (accessed Jan. 23, 2009).
"Nancy Brinker: She's Racing Toward a Cure." Aug. 29, 1999. *JournalStar.*
   www2.pjstar.com/index.php/legacy/article/nancy_brinker_shes_racing_
   toward_a_cure/ (accessed Jan. 24, 2009).
Reiter, Amy. "A Pink Badge of Courage." Sept./Oct. 2004. University of Illinois
   Alumni Association at Urbana. www.uiaa.org/urbana/illinoisalumni/
   utxt0405d.html (accessed Jan. 23, 2009).
"The Susan G. Komen Breast Cancer Foundation." Answers.com. www.answers
   .com/topic/susan-g-komen-breast-cancer-foundation (accessed Jan. 24, 2009).
Tresniowski, Alex. "Promise Kept." Oct. 29, 2001. *People.* www.people.com/
   people/archive/article/0,20135585,00.html.

38. Starbucks

Ayres, Chris. "Starbucks Logo Too Hot for Customers." May 30, 2008. *Time.*
   www.time.com/time/subscriber/2004/time100/builders/100schultz.html
   (accessed June 8, 2008).

"Howard Schultz." 2008. Wikipedia. http://en.wikipedia.org/wiki/Howard_
Schultz.

Kiviat, Barbara. "Selling Latte to the Masses." April 18, 2004. *Time*. www.time
.com/time/subscriber/2004/time100/builders/100schultz.html (accessed
June 8, 2008).

Schorn, Daniel. "Howard Schultz: The Star of Starbucks." April 23, 2006.
CBSNews. www.cbsnews.com/stories/2006/04/21/60minutes/main
1532246.shtml (accessed June 8, 2008).

39. Amazon.com

"Jeff Bezos." 2008. Wikipedia. http://en.wikipedia.org/wiki/Jeff_Bezos.

"Jeff Bezos." Answers.com. www.answers.com/topic/jeff-bezos (accessed Dec.
23, 2008).

"Jeff Bezos." Entrepreneur.com. www.entrepreneur.com/article/printthis/
197608.html (accessed Dec. 23, 2008).

"Jeff Bezos." NationMaster.com. www.nationmaster.com/encyclopedia/Jeff
-Bezos (accessed Dec. 23, 2008).

"Jeff Bezos." NNDB. www.nndb.com/people/436/000022370 (accessed Dec. 23,
2008).

"Jeff Bezos Biography." Biography.com. www.biography.com/articles/Jeff-Bezos
-37251 (accessed Dec. 23, 2008).

"Jeffrey P. Bezos." Academy of Achievement.
www.achievement.org/autodoc/page/bez0bio-1 (accessed Dec. 23, 2008).

Quittner, Josh. "The Charmed Life of Amazon's Jeff Bezos." April 15, 2008. CNN.
http://money.cnn.com/2008/04/14/news/companies/quittner_bezos
.fortune/index.htm (accessed Dec. 22, 2008).

40. Netflix

Abkowitz, Alyssa. "How Netflix Got Started." Jan. 28, 2009. *CNN Money*.
http://money.cnn.com/2009/01/27/news/newsmakers/hastings_netflix
.fortune (accessed June 10, 2009).

"Alum Reed Hastings (MA '98): The Brain Behind Netflix." Dec. 3, 2006. *CBS News*.
http://ed.stanford.edu/suse/news-bureau/displayRecord.php?tablename
=susenews&id=217 (accessed June 11, 2009).

Block, Alex Ben. "Reed Hastings: Innovator of the Year." March 29, 2009. *Hollywood Reporter*. www.hollywoodreporter.com/hr/special-reports/reed
-hastings-innovator-of-the-year-1003956632.story (accessed June 11, 2009).

Brennan, Carol. "Reed Hastings Biography." 2008. Notable Biographies.
www.notablebiographies.com/newsmakers2/2006-Ei-La/Hastings-Reed
.html (accessed June 10, 2009).

Hamilton, Joan. "Netflix Founder Reed Hastings (AM '98) Featured in Stanford Magazine." Jan./Feb. 2006. *Stanford Magazine*. http://ed.stanford.edu/suse/news-bureau/displayRecord.php?tablename=susenews&id=139 (accessed June 10, 2009).

Hopkins, Jim. "'Charismatic' Founder Keeps Netflix Adapting." April 24, 2006. *USA Today*. www.usatoday.com/money/companies/management/2006-04-23-exec-ceo-profile-netflix_x.htm (accessed June 10, 2009).

Kane, Mondo. "He Got Mail!" Jan. 24, 2009. DVD Town. http://board.dvdtown.com/news/he-got-mail—how-reed-hastings-revolutionized-the-movie-rental-business-with-netflix/6344 (accessed June 10, 2009).

Kiviat, Barbara. "Reed Hastings." April 10, 2005. *Time*. www.time.com/time/magazine/article/0,9171,1047448,00.html (accessed June 10, 2009).

"Reed Hastings." 2009. Wikipedia. http://en.wikipedia.org/wiki/Reed_Hastings.

Schorn, Daniel. "The Brain Behind Netflix." Dec. 3, 2006. *CBS News*. www.cbsnews.com/stories/2006/12/01/60minutes/main2222059.shtml (accessed June 10, 2009).

Wagner, Mary. "Light Bulb Moment." Feb. 2007. Internet Retailer. www.internetretailer.com/internet/marketing-conference/63265-light-bulb-moment.html (accessed June 10, 2009).

Zipkin, Amy. "Out of Africa, onto the Web." Dec. 17, 2006. *New York Times*. www.nytimes.com/2006/12/17/jobs/17boss.html (accessed June 11, 2009).

Acknowledgments

The most revised page in a manuscript is the acknowledgments page. I discovered this when I wrote the one for *Zelda*. I constantly changed it, depending on the ebb and flow of my interpersonal relationships. However, there are some individuals who never have to fear the Delete button, and they are as follows.

The first person I want to mention is Caren Johnson, my literary agent, without whom *Zelda* would have remained only the name of Fitzgerald's wife. When she emailed me the news that *Eureka!* had been accepted for publication, there was jumping on both the East and the West coasts.

Without Meg Leder, my editor at Perigee, my books would have remained in the realm of dreams associated with pipes. Writing is my second career and my first love, and Meg turned it into a reality. One of my favorite memories is when Caren, Meg, and I had lunch together in Greenwich Village. When I return to the East Coast to speak at Yale University Library (my first time in an institution whose walls are associated with ivy), I hope we can take that opportunity to reunite. I am also looking forward, at that time, to meeting in person Avis Weeks, a resident of New Jersey (who has the distinction of having gone to school with Philip Roth). We connected when she read *Zelda* and emailed me, telling of her desire that someone dedicate a book to her. She lamented that all her two former husbands ever penned were lists.

In order for there to be a second book, the first one must do well, and any success *Zelda* enjoyed can be attributed to Catherine Milne, who was my publicist at that time. She has since become a law student at Cornell; in return for writing her a letter of recommendation, she promised that when she graduated, she would offer me a lifetime of pro bono work, on the contingency that I am compelled to commit any random acts of madness.

I would also like to thank Stephen Scanlon for his excellent work on the bibliographies for both books. There was a lot of shuffling of boxes of documents between his classroom and mine. Another teacher I would like to thank is Nancy Hokenson, who apparently does not subscribe to the Gore Vidal quotation, "Every time a friend succeeds something in me dies." Her joy in *Zelda*'s success was, if not as great as mine, not a far second. Other Sweetwater High School staff who offered encouragement or came to my Barnes & Noble book signing in a show of solidarity were Laura Charles, Meg Garcia, Donna Mulrean, Eric Esperon, Debbie Domenie, Jill Shapira-Norcross, Vicki Urias, Michael Garcia, Jerome Kocher, Yolanda Rocha, Reid Burns, Ivy Callaway, Maureen Rymer, Robert Bonilla, Georgia Wapnowski, Scott Grover, Kevin Smith, Nancy Garcia, Alan Nakano, Diane Rider, and Michelle Brunkow.

The alma mater of Sweetwater High School, where I teach in National City, California, states, "Where e'er we may roam / In our hearts, SUHI LIVES!" In a similar vein, though I have roamed from my native Toronto, Canada, some individuals still make it the place Dorothy Gale referred to as "no place like home." Whenever I return, I am given a warm reception by my cousins Alan and Brenda Vernon and Elisa Landau. I also want to acknowledge my new nephew, Vida Shale Wagman; I hope he will grow up to be as unique as his name.

More than a passing nod to Kane Handel, who despite being the mother of three and an attorney, always found time to offer both encouragement and feedback. I enjoyed the evening when I spoke to her book club, Le Mot Juste, a French expression meaning "the right wording." (The name reminds me of the Mark Twain quotation, "The difference between the right word and the almost right word is the difference between lightning and a lightning bug.") I also enjoyed her suggestions for my next book on how famous lovers met—so much so that I'm working on it now.

Similarly, my appreciation goes to Victoria Wooden of San Francisco, who I had the fortune to meet through *Zelda*.

My family, my emotional North Star, deserves my most heartfelt appreciation. Thank you to my husband, Joel, who had to hear the dirt on every dedication and had to hear about each and every eureka moment. (He is actively seeking a support group for husbands of wives who are writers.) I hope this was due to interest rather than the fact that California is a community-property state. I also appreciate his understanding that having a full-time teaching job and writing leaves me no time to be a domestic diva. Suffice it to say, a plaque in my home could read, "Martha Stewart doesn't live here." It is also because I do not cook that I appreciate Bill and Nadine Matthews inviting us to holiday dinners. Their hospitality makes us feel less like strangers in a strange land. I also want to acknowledge my daughter, Jordanna (Jordi), who is not just a daughter but, in her text language, my BFF. My mother, Gilda Wagman, pre-publication, believed in *Zelda* and *"Erika,"* as she refers to *Eureka!* in her Brazilian accent. My deepest gratitude belongs to Bill Wiener, who was like a son to my mother to help compensate for her absent daughter.

Lastly, I want to pay tribute to the individuals mentioned in *Eureka!* whose moments transformed our world from black-and-white to Technicolor.

May we all have our eureka moment . . .

Love,
Marlene

water kayaking at the time, and in kayaking if you stare and focus on the problem you are more likely to hit danger. I focused on the safe water and what I wanted to happen. I didn't listen to the skeptics." This proved a sound decision, as his company was acquired by Rational Software for $750 million.

Most people who receive close to a billion dollars would rest on their laurels, but Reed Hastings was not most people. He felt he was still too young and too hungry for intellectual stimulation to become a denizen of the dot-com idle rich.

In 1998, Reed was irritated when he misplaced his video rental of *Apollo 13*. When he finally returned it, six weeks late, he was charged a late fee of $40. He recalled that he was reluctant to mention this to his wife, who would respond with an eye roll, "an eye roll that could kill." The unfairness of paying four times the amount of a product's value did not sit well with him.

Later, at the gym, he realized the health club had a much better business model. For a set cost of $30 a month, one could work out as little or as much as one wanted. This led to Hastings' eureka moment: He could start a video rental company where, for a membership, one could check out movies and not be charged any of the hated late fees.

Serendipity stepped in at this point when a friend told him about a new technology called DVD. This got Reed thinking of a new twist to his plan: With the slimmer version, perhaps customers could be mailed movies; thus, he could start a business that would not just end late fees but end the trip to the video store altogether. He ran to Tower Records and purchased a bunch of CDs and mailed them to himself, then anxiously waited to see what condition they would arrive in.

When he tore open the package and saw them in pristine condition, he knew he had hit upon technological gold.

Hastings recalled a time when he had lived in England and the local residents would leave out their empty milk bottles to be replaced with full ones by the milkman. He decided to build his startup company after that model: When one home-delivered movie was returned, another one would be sent. He did not name his company "DVD by Mail" because, in true visionary fashion, he foresaw that in the modern age, the only constant is change, and that one day the DVD would go the way of the VHS. Hence the name, Netflix. The formula proved an irresistible carrot to customers.

Today, the company complex is a 165,000-square-foot Tuscan-style warehouse situated in Los Gatos, on the edge of Silicon Valley. The warehouse stores a staggering 26 million DVDs, far more than could be obtained by even the most gargantuan of video stores. Netflix sends out more than 1.5 million of their red envelopes per day, making the company one of the post office's top ten customers for first-class mail.

Reed remains as socially minded as most billionaires are money minded. He donated $1 million to open a charter school and was president of the California State Board of Education.

Los Gatos, where Netflix is headquartered, can serve as a symbolic name for the company's CEO, for he has lived if not nine lives, at least several: Peace Corps volunteer, Stanford graduate student, multimillionaire executive, philanthropist, and family man. Thanks to his eureka, Americans can embark on armchair adventures merely by opening a ubiquitous red envelope.

7. The Nobel Prize

"Alfred Nobel." 2002. *Nordic Way*. www.nordicway.com/search/Sweden/sweden_alfred_nobel.htm (accessed July 3, 2008).

"Alfred Nobel." 2008. Wikipedia. http://en.wikipedia.org/wiki/Alfred_Nobel.

"Alfred Nobel." Dimdima. http://dimdima.com/science/science_common/show_science.asp?q_aid=32&q_title=Alfred+Nobel (accessed July 3, 2008).

"Alfred Nobel: The Man Behind the Prizes, His Life and Work." Oct. 2008. *The Free Library*. www.thefreelibrary.com/Alfred+Nobel:+The+Man+Behind+the+Prizes+His+Life+and+Work-a079254315 (accessed July 3, 2008).

Altman, Lawrence K. "Alfred Nobel and the Prize That Almost Didn't Happen." Sept. 26, 2006. *New York Times*. www.nytimes.com/2006/09/26/health/26docs.html (accessed July 3, 2008).

Campbell, James. "Alfred Nobel and His Prizes." *Boston Review*. http://bostonreview.net/BR26.5/campbell.html (accessed July 3, 2008).

"Nobel Prize." 2008. Wikipedia. http://en.wikipedia.org/wiki/Nobel_Prize.

Rosenberg, Jennifer. "History of the Nobel Prizes." About.com. http://history1900s.about.com/od/medicaladvancesissues/a/nobelhistory.htm (accessed July 3, 2008).

Rowen, Beth. "Nobel Prize History." 2007. Information Please Database. www.infoplease.com/spot/nobel-prize-history.html (accessed June 30, 2008).

8. Chiropractic

Butler, Allen. "Daniel David Palmer and the Origins of Chiropractic Medicine." Aug. 28, 2007. Associated Press. www.associatedcontent.com/article/357784/daniel_david_palmer_and_the_origins.html (accessed June 1, 2009).

"Chiropractic History." 2009. Wikipedia. http://en.wikipedia.org/wiki/Chiropractic_history.

"Chiropractic History." Oohoi.com. www.oohoi.com/physical_therapy/chiropractic/history.htm (accessed June 1, 2009).

"Chiropractic History." Sherman College of Straight Chiropractic. www.sherman.edu/edu/visitors/chirohistory.asp (accessed June 1, 2009).

Cooksey, Gloria. "Daniel David Palmer." Answers.com. www.answers.com/topic/daniel-david-palmer (accessed June 1, 2009).

"D.D. Palmer." Advancing Chiropractic. www.advancingchiropractic.com/index.php?file=ddpalmer.html (accessed June 1, 2009).

"Daniel David Palmer." AbsoluteAstronomy.com. www.absoluteastronomy.com/topics/Daniel_David_Palmer (accessed June 1, 2009).

"Daniel David Palmer" 2009. Wikipedia. http://en.wikipedia.org/wiki/Daniel_David_Palmer.

Dorausch, Michael. "Daniel David Palmer and Chiropractic Founders Day 2008."

"History of Kentucky Derby." May 1, 2009. www.thelifeofluxury.com/history-of
-the-kentucky-derby/ (accessed May 22, 2009).

Holmberg, James. "The Clark Family and the Kentucky Derby." The Filson Historical Society. www.filsonhistorical.org/news_v4n1_clarkderby.html
(accessed May 14, 2009).

"Kentucky Derby." 2009. Wikipedia. http://en.wikipedia.org/wiki/Kentucky_Derby.

"Kentucky Derby." GetMeIn. www.getmein.com/horse-racing/kentucky-derby
-tickets.html (accessed May 14, 2009).

"The Kentucky Derby—A History." May 4, 2008. *Allied Equine.* www.alliedequine
.com/the-kentucky-derby-a-history/325/ (accessed May 14, 2009).

"Kentucky Derby History." 2009. TicketCity. www.ticketcity.com/horse-racing
-tickets/kentucky-derby-tickets.html (accessed May 14, 2009).

Melikov, Greg. "Welcome to Kentucky Derby Trivia." http://nationalsportsreview
.com/sports/us/horseracing/2009/04/27/welcome-to-kentucky-derby-trivia
-%E2%80%93-try-your-luck (accessed May 14, 2009).

"Meriwether Lewis Clark Jr." 2009. Wikipedia. http://en.wikipedia.org/wiki/Meri
wether-Lewis-Clark,_Jr.

"Meriwether Lewis Clark, Jr." NationMaster.com. www.nationmaster.com/ency
clopedia/Meriwether-Lewis-Clark,-Jr. (accessed May 14, 2009).

Powers, Rita. "The Kentucky Derby: A Historical Look at Horse Racing's Finest."
http://petcaretips.net/history-kentucky-derby.html (accessed May 15, 2009).

"A Review of the Kentucky Derby Festival." April 10, 2009. Associated Content.
www.associatedcontent.com/article/1609634/a_review_of_the_kentucky
_derby_festival.html?cat=2 (accessed May 14, 2009).

5. Woolworth's

"F. W. Woolworth Company." 2008. Wikipedia. http://en.wikipedia.org/wiki/F.W.
_Woolworth_Company.

"Franklin Winfield Woolworth." 2008. Wikipedia. http://en.wikipedia.org/wiki/
Frank_Woolworth.

6. The Olympic Games

"Pierre de Coubertin." 2008. Wikipedia. http://en.wikipedia.org/wiki/Pierre_
de_Coubertin.

"Pierre de Coubertin." UXL Encyclopedia of World Biography. FindArticles.com.
http://findarticles.com/p/articles/mi_gx5229/is_2003/ai_n19152054
(accessed March 1, 2009).

Downey, Lynn. "History of Blue Jeans." Jeans and Accessories. www.jeans -and-accessories.com/history-of-blue-jeans.html (accessed June 10, 2008).

"Levi Strauss." 2000. Davitt. www.germanheritage.com/biographies/mtoz/ strauss.html (accessed June 10, 2008).

"Levi Strauss." *Who Made America?* www.pbs.org/wgbh/theymadeamerica/who made/strauss_lo.html (accessed June 11, 2008).

Lohmann, Birgit. "Denim." 2000. Designboom. www.designboom.com/eng/edu cation/denim2.html (accessed June 10, 2008).

Ross, Andrew (ed.). "A History of Denim." Encyclopedia Britannica. www.newint .org/issue302/blue.htm (accessed June 10, 2008).

Uher, Pam. "Origins: Blue Jeans." Helium. www.helium.com/items/996835 -origins-blue-jeans (accessed June 11, 2008).

Weber, Caroline. "Reviews: Jeans." Aug. 18, 2006. *International Herald Tribune*. www.iht.com/articles/2006/08/18/arts/idbriefs19E.php (accessed June 11, 2008).

4. The Kentucky Derby

"About Churchill Downs." Kentucky Derby. www.kentuckyderby.com/2009/about -churchill (accessed May 14, 2009).

Brodowsky, Pamela, and Tom Philbin. *Two Minutes to Glory*. New York: Churchill Downs, 2006.

"Churchill Downs, the Kentucky Derby, and Louisville." March 2, 2003. www0 .epinions.com/review/trvl-Dest-United_States-Kentucky-Churchill_Downs/ content_91652394628 (accessed May 14, 2009).

Crawford, Amy. "Derby Days." May 1, 2007. Smithsonian. www.smithsonianmag .com/travel/derby_days.html (accessed May 14, 2009).

Elliott, Jessica. "Kentucky Derby Facts and History." About.com. http://louisville .about.com/od/attractionsevents/p/kentuckyderby.htm (accessed May 14, 2009).

"Evolution of the Derby." BetTheDerby.com. www.betthederby.com/evolution-of -the-kentucky-derby.html (accessed May 14, 2009).

Ewing, Rex A. "The First." www.pixyjackpress.com/pdf/thefirstkentuckyderby.pdf.

Griffith, Benjamin. "Kentucky Derby." http://findarticles.com/p/articles/mi_glepc /is_tov/ai_2419100671 (accessed May 14, 2009).

Hillenbrand, Laura. "The Derby." May/June 1999. *American Heritage*. www.amer icanheritage.com/articles/magazine/ah/1999/3/1999_3_98.shtml (accessed May 14, 2009).

"The History of Churchill Downs and the Kentucky Derby." 2009. www.kentucky derbytickets2007.com/kentucky-derby-churchill-downs-history.asp (ac- cessed May 14, 2009).

Resources

1. "Amazing Grace"

"Amazing Grace." 2008. Wikipedia. http://en.wikipedia.org/wiki/Amazing_
  Grace.

"John Newton." 2008. Wikipedia. http://en.wikipedia.org/wiki/John_Newton.

Rogers, Al. "Amazing Grace: The Story of John Newton." Aug. 1996. *Away Here in
  Texas.* www.anointedlinks.com/amazing_grace.html (accessed Sept. 28,
  2008).

2. Madame Tussauds

"Madame Tussauds." 2008. Wikipedia. http://en.wikipedia.org/wiki/Madame_
  Tussauds.

"Marie Tussaud." 2008. Wikipedia. http://en.wikipedia.org/wiki/Marie_Tussaud.

Ogintz, Eileen. "Madame Tussaud's in London: Something for Everyone in the
  Family." 1998. *Los Angeles Times.* www.familytravelnetwork.com/articles/kdz
  _madametaussad.asp (accessed May 17, 2008).

3. Levi's

Ament, Phil. "Jacob Davis." July 28, 2006. The Great Idea Finder. www.ideafinder
  .com/history/inventors/davis.htm (accessed June 9, 2008).

Brody, Seymour. "Levi Strauss: The Originator of Levi's." Oct. 18, 2006. *Jewish
  Heroes and Heroines in America.* www.fau.edu/library/brody22.htm
  (accessed June 10, 2008).

Caro, Joe. "Levis: The Jeans That Won the West." About.com. http://collect
  ibles.about.com/od/cowboyheroes/a/joecarolevi.htm (accessed June 10,
  2008).

"Denim History." Azure Chic. www.azurechic.com/site/index.cfm?display=77800
  (accessed June 10, 2008).

"Denim Jeans." Small Town. http://smalltownjeans.com/jeans/designer_jean
  .html (accessed June 10, 2008).

Dorfman, Marjorie. "Blue Jeans: An American Phenomenon." Pop Goes the Culture. www.cultureschlockonline.com/Articles/jeans.html (accessed June 10,
  2008).

- Netflix offered a $1 million prize to anyone who could develop a personalization engine to improve the accuracy of its movie recommendations by at least 10 percent.
- Hastings admits he still frequents an old-school DVD store when he wants a movie the same day.
- Hastings was elected to the Microsoft board of directors.
- Hastings says he has seen over a thousand films, and the one that impacted him most was *Sophie's Choice.*
- The Netflix warehouse opens at 4 a.m.